Climate Action for Kids

An Introduction to Climate Change

ACKNOWLEDGMENTS

To my mother, for teaching me to care deeply about the world around me, and to my father, for teaching me the power of words to make change.

To everyone who has worked tirelessly on climate solutions, proving every day the importance of never giving up.

Edited by Andrew Mollenkof and Brett Ortler

Cover and book design by Jonathan Norberg

Proofread by Jenna Barron

Cover images used under license from Shutterstock.com:
FRONT: **Gorynvd:** picking garbage; **MEE KO DONG:** hand & plant; **Najmi Arif:** leaf dew drop; **Porstocker:** earth; **Vlad Ra27:** recycling logo; BACK: **Ortis:** leaves; **kubai:** water droplet.

Images copyright of their prospective photographers:
Dean Maupin: 160; **NASA Goddard Space Flight Center:** 51; **NASA Goddard Space Flight Center/ Ludovic Brucker:** 44; **NOAA data:** 144; and **Brett Ortler:** 148.

Images used under license from Shutterstock.com:
24K-Production: 8; **Aaaarianne:** 147; **Abdul Razak Latif:** 11 (bottom); **Adwo:** 86; **aerophoto:** 65; **Ahanov Michael:** 27 (top); **Akhdian Reppawali:** 34; **Alan Budman:** 116 (middle); **Alaskagirl8821:** 110; **alicja neumiler:** 124; **ANATOLY Foto:** 22; **andreonegin:** 69; **anto.cakep:** 32 (bottom); **apiguide:** 85 (top); **BearFotos:** 125 (bottom); **Bernhard Staehli:** 113 (bottom); **BEST-BACKGROUNDS:** 53, 103; **Bilanol:** 55 (bottom, solar); **Bjorn H Stuedal:** 9; **BlueRingMedia:** 119; **Bmphotographer:** 80; **brichuas:** 13; **Bryant B:** 77; **buttchi 3 Sha Life:** 117 (top); **Carolin Wygant:** 116 (bottom); **Catwalk-Photos:** 37 (top); **Chatchawal Phumkaew:** 128 (top); **Chris Curtis:** 15 (bottom); **Chris J Bradshaw:** 54; **Cid Guedes:** 102 (bottom); **Cinar12345:** 23 (bottom); **CL Shebley:** 127 (top); **Dalibor Danilovic:** 37 (middle); **David Pereiras:** 112 (bottom); **Delpixel:** 12 (bottom); **Dennis Wegewijs:** 87; **Designua:** 16 (bottom), 23 (both); **Desire Le Roux 1111:** 105; **DimaBerlin:** 138; **Dollar Mom:** 36 (top); **DONG-SEUN YANG:** 17; **Dragon Images:** 108; **Drone Motion Stock:** 55 (top, nuclear); **Elizaveta Galitckaia:** 48; **Evgenii Bakhchev:** 76 (top); **Evgeny_V:** 55 (bottom, hydropower); **Fahroni:** 73; **fizkes:** 139 (top); **fotogurmespb:** 102 (top); **Fotokostic:** 26, 83 (bottom); **freedomnaruk:** 98; **Garsya:** 92 (bottom); **George Trumpeter:** 12 (top); **Gorodenkoff:** 111; **haafitte:** 62; **Heather Appert:** 146 (right); **Heidi Besen:** 115; **HRFN:** 96; **hrui:** 76 (bottom); **IlyaMatushkin:** 21; **India Picture:** 133; **Jacob Lund:** 141; **JacobLoyacano:** 118; **Jacopo Landi:** 74 (bottom); **Jane Rix:** 121 (bottom); **Jasmine Sahin:** 146 (left); **JDzacovsky:** 97; **Jenya Smyk:** 93 (top), 94; **Jess Lang:** 122 (top); **Johan Larson:** 84 (top); **Jonah Lange:** 104; **joserpizarro:** 114; **JSpataro:** 151; **Karlie Butler:** 25 (top right); **KatMoys:** 127 (bottom);

Credits continued on page 160

10 9 8 7 6 5 4 3 2 1
Climate Action for Kids: An Introduction to Climate Change
Copyright © 2026 by Ian Hunt
Published by Adventure Publications, an imprint of AdventureKEEN
310 Garfield Street South
Cambridge, Minnesota 55008
(800) 678-7006
adventurepublications.net
All rights reserved
Printed in China
Library of Congress Control Number: 2025949809
ISBN 978-1-64755-447-7 (pbk.); 978-1-64755-448-4 (ebook)

Climate Action for Kids

An Introduction to Climate Change

Ian Hunt

Adventure Publications

Table of Contents

ACKNOWLEDGMENTS 2

INTRODUCTION: EARTH 9
- What is Climate? 10
- Weather vs. Climate...........................12
- The Atmosphere 13
- The "Spheres" 14
- Law of Conservation of Matter 17
- The Carbon Cycle.............................18
- The Greenhouse Effect 22
- Linking Carbon and Warming 28
- Carbon Sources and Sinks.....................31
- Net-Zero.................................... 34
- Industry Greenhouse Emissions................ 35
- Global Climate Emissions 39

HOW WE KNOW................................ 43
- Ice Cores.................................... 43
- Sampling the Atmosphere 44
- Measuring Other Parts of the Earth........... 45
- Effects on Different Species.................. 46

ARE WE THE PROBLEM? 48

CLIMATE ACTION NEEDS EVERYONE............. 49

BIG PROBLEMS REQUIRE BIG SOLUTIONS 51
- A Hole in the Sky: How We Helped the Ozone Layer 51

A FIELD GUIDE TO CLIMATE CHANGE CAUSES (AND SOLUTIONS) **54**

Energy Sources **56**
Non-Renewable Energy 57
Coal.. 58
Oil 60
Gas 62
Nuclear..................................... 64
Solutions: Renewable Energy 66
Solar Energy................................ 68
Wind Energy.................................72
Hydropower.................................76
Geothermal Energy 78
Biomass 80

Destruction of Nature......................... **82**
Agriculture.................................... 82
Forestry 84
Land-Use Change............................. 85
Solutions: Working with Nature 87

Industrial Emissions and Damage............... **88**
Solutions: Technology and Using Less 89

Transportation **90**
Solutions: Designing Well and Electric Tech 91

Waste.. **93**
Solutions: Using Less, Reusing More, and the Circular Economy 94

CLIMATE IMPACTS (AND SOLUTIONS).............. **98**

Wild Weather................................ **100**
Heatwaves 100
Safety During Heatwaves....................101

Droughts..101
   Safety During Droughts 102
Floods 102
   Safety During Floods 103
Hurricanes 103
   Safety During Hurricanes.................... 104
Tornadoes 104
   Safety During Tornadoes....................105
Hailstorms......................................105
   Safety During Hailstorms 106
Blizzards and Freezes........................ 106
   Safety During Blizzards and Freezes 106
Creating Resilience for Severe Weather........107

OTHER CLIMATE IMPACTS 110

Wildfires 110
Solutions 111
Melting Ice 113
Solutions 114
Ocean Rise 115
Solutions 116
Ocean Acidification 117
Solutions 118
Current Loss 119
Solutions 120
Biodiversity Loss 121
Solutions 122
Food Loss 124
Solutions 125
Freshwater Loss............................. 126
Solutions 127

Health Impacts **128**
  Solutions 129
 Climate Justice **130**
  Solutions 131

WHAT CAN I DO? 132
 Debunking Common Myths About Climate 132
  "Isn't the Climate Always Changing?"...........133
  "Isn't it the Sun?" 135
  "What About the Scientists
    Who Don't Agree?"..........................136
 Taking Care of Yourself and Others.......... **138**
  How to Handle Hard Topics....................138
  Looking Out for Your Neighbors...............139
  Small Steps Every Day........................140

ACTIVITIES 142
 Community Science 142
 Measuring Climate Through Crafts........... **143**
 Imagine a Better Future:
 What Could Go Here? **146**
 Joining a Community Garden 147
 Calculate Your Energy Use **148**
 Climate Survey **149**
 Create Positive Land Use Change!............. **151**
 Start a Group 152

SOURCES.................................. 153
GLOSSARY................................. 154
ABOUT THE AUTHOR....................... 160

Introduction: Earth

The Earth is a special place. Earth's systems keep us alive and comfortable. They provide fresh water, clean air, comfortable temperatures, healthy food, and safe places to live. And life is everywhere on Earth, from the highest mountains to the deepest oceans.

Life on Earth does its best when the planet's systems are totally balanced. Humans, plants, animals, fungi, and other life forms all depend on the Earth's systems being in harmony.

Right now, the Earth's systems are not in balance, leading to climate change. Climate change has started to cause big problems all over the world. These problems affect the systems that provide the fresh water, clean air, and comfortable temperatures life depends on.

In this book, we will explore how the Earth's balance has been disturbed. Understanding how climate change started, and how it affects us, will help us respond to the problems it's causing, as well as help prevent it from getting worse.

Climate change can be scary to talk and think about, but people have a lot of power to make things better for generations to come. And you can help too!

WHAT IS CLIMATE?

The Earth's **climate** is what makes life possible on Earth. **Climate** refers to a consistent set of conditions that are present, globally, on Earth for a long period of time, including the mix of gases in the atmosphere *(say it, at-mos-feer)* and the normal ranges for temperature, rain, pressure, and wind.

The Earth's climate keeps everything not too hot and not too cold. Earth's climate is the reason why water can be liquid on Earth, not frozen solid or heated to a gas. Earth's climate helps life thrive. Since it keeps the temperature just right for life to exist, some people call Earth the "Goldilocks Planet" as it's "just right" for water, and life.

Climate is what makes places like Florida warm and tropical, and places like Arizona dry and hot. The climate is how we know crops like to grow in California, and to carry an umbrella if you live in the state of Washington.

While it seems like climate just affects the weather, think about how much the weather impacts daily life. The food we eat was grown in areas that provide enough sun and rain to grow them. We choose the clothes we buy based on the weather where we live. Where and how we build our houses and cities is decided by the area's climate. The climate we live in determines a lot of our lives, but it's usually not something we think about. In this book, we will explore what climate change is, why it's occurring, and what we can do to protect the Earth from changing for the worse.

WEATHER VS. CLIMATE

What is the difference between weather and climate? The two overlap, but there is a very simple way to tell the difference between weather and climate: time.

Weather is what is going on in the atmosphere during a short period of time. You probably know that the weather can change multiple times a day. A day can start out cloudy in the morning, rain at noon, and be sunny in the evening. That's all weather. Weather can happen over hours, days, weeks, or even seasons.

Climate, on the other hand, is the average of all the weather over a long period of time. For example, for the past 50 years, it has been warm and sunny in San Diego, California. So, the climate of that area over the last 50 years has been a warm, dry climate.

Scientists sometimes define the climate of a region using all the records that they have of that area. But it is also possible to talk about the climate of an area using a shorter or specific time frame. For example, scientists might want to look at an area's climate over a 30-year time period instead of something longer. For areas where the climate has shifted, looking at the climate over both long and short amounts of time can give valuable information.

THE ATMOSPHERE

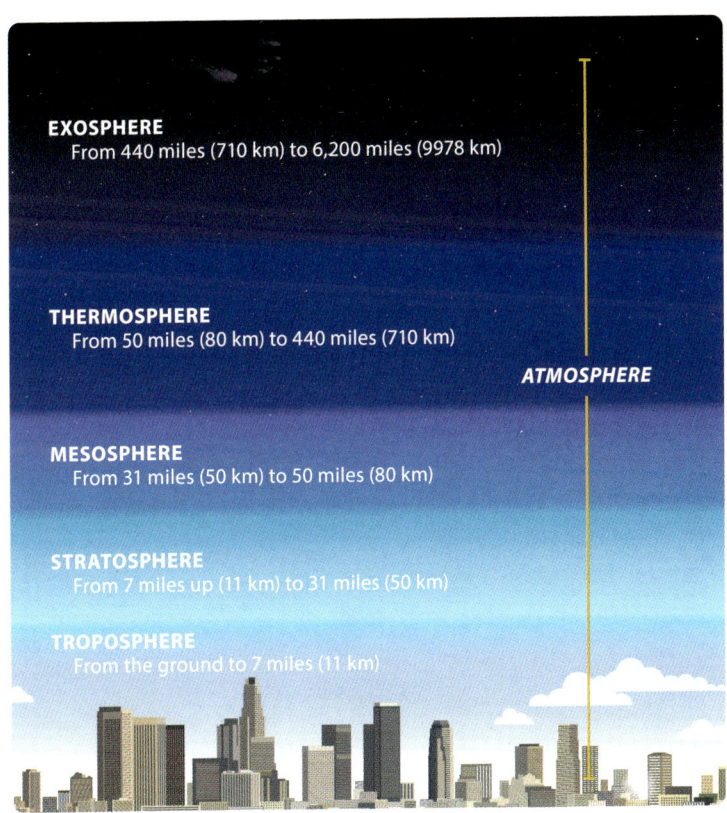

EXOSPHERE
From 440 miles (710 km) to 6,200 miles (9978 km)

THERMOSPHERE
From 50 miles (80 km) to 440 miles (710 km)

ATMOSPHERE

MESOSPHERE
From 31 miles (50 km) to 50 miles (80 km)

STRATOSPHERE
From 7 miles up (11 km) to 31 miles (50 km)

TROPOSPHERE
From the ground to 7 miles (11 km)

THE "SPHERES"

The atmosphere is one of the main reasons life exists on Earth, but there are a lot of other systems on Earth that make life possible and are "just right" for us to survive and be comfortable. These systems are all linked together. We can call these five systems "the spheres."

Atmosphere The atmosphere is a layer of invisible gases that shields us from harmful UV rays from the sun, lets us breathe, and keeps the Earth warm enough for life. Life as we know it can't exist without an atmosphere. For example, the moon doesn't have an atmosphere, and its daily temperatures range between -230 degrees Fahrenheit and +250 degrees F. The atmosphere covers the entirety of the surface of the Earth, and it is where Earth is experiencing the biggest problems with carbon imbalance and climate change.

Hydrosphere The hydrosphere *(say it, hi-dro-sfeer)* contains all the water on Earth. This includes the clouds (which are made of water vapor *(say it, vay-por)*, rain, oceans, lakes, and rivers, and groundwater systems.

Cryosphere The cryosphere *(say it, cry-oh-sfeer)* is similar to the hydrosphere, but it includes all of the ice on the planet. There is a lot of overlap between the hydrosphere and the cryosphere, since ice is just frozen water, but there are some services that are unique to each one. For example, the cryophere's white surfaces reflect sunlight back into space, while much of the water in the hydrosphere absorbs sunlight.

Lithosphere The lithosphere *(say it, lith-oh-sfeer)* contains all the solid rock and earth on the planet. This includes all the space between the crust of the Earth and the Earth's core.

Biosphere The biosphere *(say it, bye-oh-sfeer)* contains all the living things on the planet. This includes plants, plankton, mammals, trees, peat moss, oysters, and even you and me.

Cryosphere

Atmosphere

Hydrosphere

Lithosphere

LAW OF CONSERVATION OF MATTER

In all the "spheres," there is a constant exchange of gases, materials, and chemicals between each other.

These systems can't create anything new, but simply move matter around, transforming old things into new things. Ice at the top of the mountain melts and flows into the river. Then the sun heats the surface of the river water, causing it to evaporate; the water molecules go from the river into the air, where later they form a cloud. The ice at the top of the mountain wasn't destroyed, but transformed, all the way into a cloud far away. This is an example of a rule of physics: the law of conservation of matter. **The Law of Conservation of Matter** states that elements (like the ice in the example) are not created or destroyed but are transformed in chemical reactions.

Get to Know Carbon and the Elements

To understand why the climate is changing, you need to know a little bit about chemical elements. Chemical elements are sort of like the building blocks of the universe. There are 118 different kinds of elements that we know about. Each element is made up of **atoms**, which are tiny particles that are in turn made up of even smaller particles: protons, neutrons, and electrons. The study of how chemical elements form and interact is called **chemistry**. And scientists have organized the 118 chemical elements based on their structure (how they are built) and properties (how they behave) in what is called the **Periodic Table**.

On Earth, some chemical elements are usually found as gases (oxygen), others are familiar metals (iron), and some can only be made in a lab (plutonium). In nature, elements can sometimes be found alone (such as a lump of pure gold), but more often than not, elements are found in **molecules**, groups of different elements that are joined together. For example, when the elements sodium and chlorine combine, they produce the compound sodium chloride (NaCl), which you probably know as table salt!

THE CARBON CYCLE

To understand climate change, you don't need to know very much chemistry. But a little bit is helpful! The image below is a carbon atom.

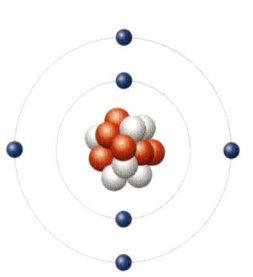

Carbon (C) is a naturally occurring element in the universe. It's also one of the main building blocks of the world around us. Through naturally occurring chemical reactions, carbon takes many different forms on our planet. You probably already know carbon but don't recognize it: The "lead" in your pencil is graphite, a type of pure carbon. Diamond is another! But more often than not, carbon is found as an "ingredient" in chemicals, including those found in plants, animals, and soil. The air that humans breathe out, carbon dioxide (CO_2), is an example!

Another way to think about the carbon atom is as if it were a world traveler. Carbon likes to explore all over the world. Carbon can be found underground, in trees, in volcanoes, in the oceans, and even on your dinner table. Carbon is everywhere, and it also often has a next destination. Scientists describe the way that it moves around the Earth in the carbon cycle.

The carbon cycle describes the process of how carbon moves between different "reservoirs," or stations, where carbon remains for a certain length of time before moving on in the cycle through a chemical change.

In the carbon cycle, when carbon enters the atmosphere, it is called a **carbon source**. When carbon is taken out of the atmosphere and stored, it is called a **carbon sink**.

Here, we can see how carbon moves through the environment, from soil, plants, and animal reservoirs, where it will remain until it moves into something else. Here is a more detailed depiction of the carbon cycle.

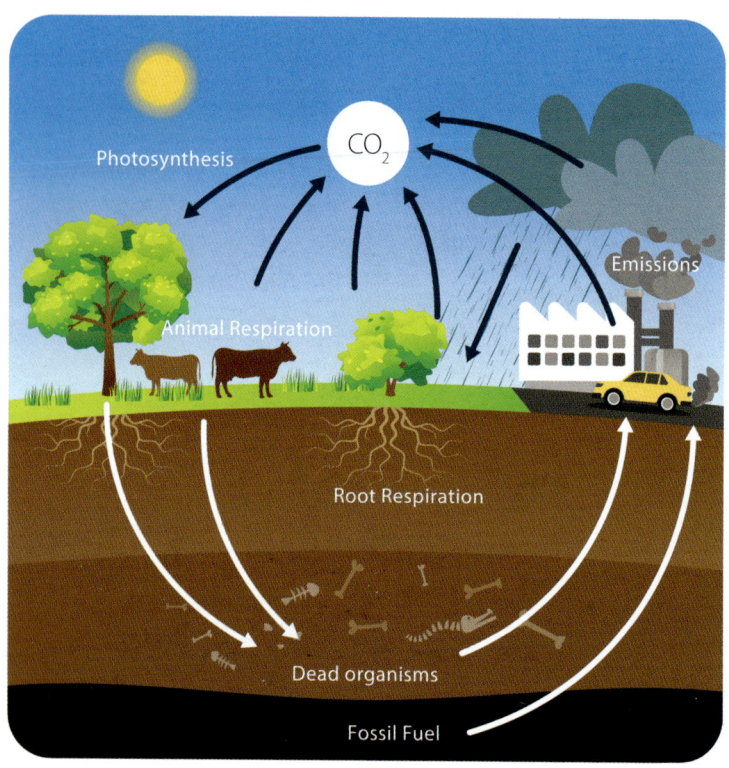

What's important to remember is that because of the law of conservation of matter, the amount of carbon on Earth does not change. However, where carbon is found is always changing. One of the main carbon "tanks" is the atmosphere, where it is found as a gas, carbon dioxide.

When humans take carbon from one tank, let's say the lithosphere, in the form of drilling oil from the ground, and move it to the atmosphere by burning the oil, scientists describe it as creating emissions. **Emissions** are when gases are released into an area where they were not before. Climate change is happening because humans have been emitting carbon into the atmosphere in the form of greenhouse gases.

THE GREENHOUSE EFFECT

Have you ever been inside a greenhouse? They are buildings made from glass, and they are warm inside, even at night or in the winter. Greenhouses take in sunlight from the outside, but the glass walls trap the sun's heat and keep it warm even when it's cool outside. The atmosphere works in the same way: Just as greenhouse glass keeps heat inside, certain gases trap heat when it tries to escape the planet, reflecting it back down to Earth's surface instead of letting it escape into space.

There are five main greenhouse gases: carbon dioxide, methane, nitrous oxide, ozone *(say it, oh-zone)*, and water vapor. A balanced mix of these gases in the atmosphere is what makes Earth the "Goldilocks Planet."

Because of these greenhouse gases, we have liquid water to drink and stable temperatures that are comfortable for human beings and other life forms on the planet. Without these greenhouse gases, the Earth would be freezing cold.

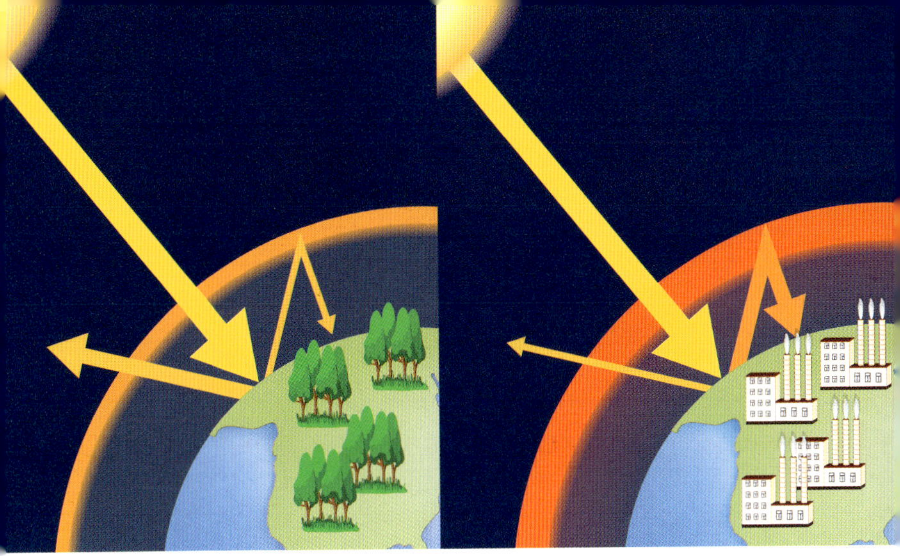

Too Many Gases

Greenhouse gases are very good at trapping the sun's heat, but over the past 200 years, we've increased the amount of greenhouse gases significantly. Adding greenhouse gases to the atmosphere has trapped extra heat in the Earth's atmosphere, leading to climate change and its resulting problems, such as unpredictable weather. This includes more-severe storms, floods, and heat waves.

Get to Know the Greenhouse Gases

Carbon dioxide, CO_2 Carbon dioxide is the most common greenhouse gas. It consists of one carbon atom and two oxygen atoms. Carbon dioxide is everywhere. It is necessary for life on Earth, but burning fossil fuels and cutting down trees, which absorb carbon dioxide, have introduced a lot of extra CO_2 into the atmosphere. The best way to get to know carbon dioxide? Take a deep breath in, and out. You just breathed out carbon dioxide. Trees and plants do the opposite; they breathe in carbon dioxide and release oxygen. Carbon dioxide lasts a long time in the atmosphere, even for hundreds of years. So, the choices we make to prevent carbon dioxide from going into the atmosphere or not matter for a long time.

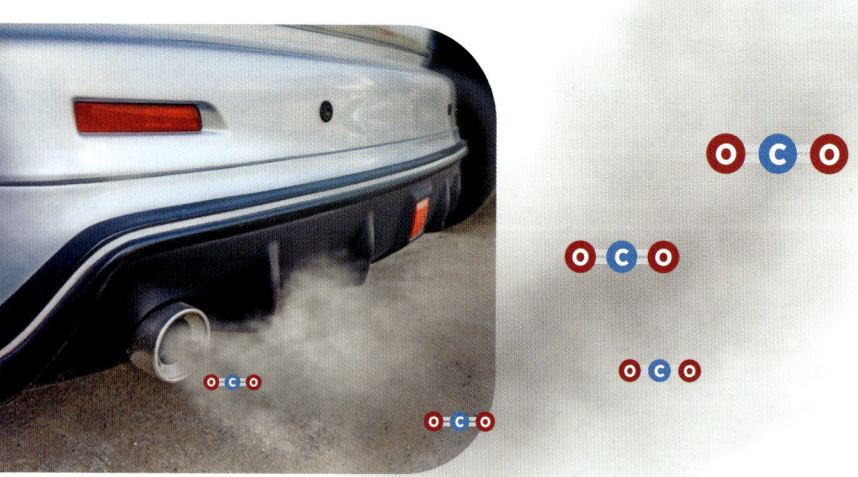

Methane, CH_4
Methane is a very powerful greenhouse gas. It is made with one carbon atom and four hydrogen atoms. Methane is 28 times more powerful at trapping heat than the same amount of carbon dioxide. Methane enters the atmosphere from many places, mostly from the production and burning of natural gas, as well as from decomposing matter, but it can also come from cows. Cows burp methane, so when they burp, they put more methane into the atmosphere. Methane also doesn't last very long in the atmosphere compared to CO_2, so even though it is more powerful, it causes warming mostly in the short term (less than 100 years) compared to carbon dioxide, which lasts longer.

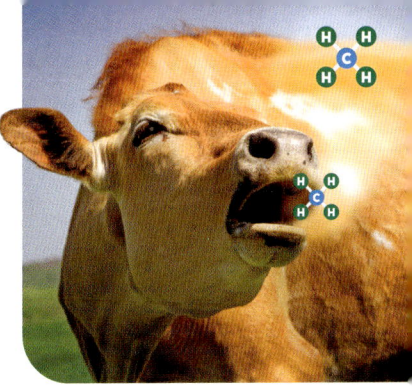

Ozone, O_3 Ozone is necessary for life on Earth. It is made with three oxygen molecules. Ozone occurs naturally at very high altitudes, where it forms the **ozone layer**. The ozone layer protects plant and animal life on Earth from harsh ultraviolet light rays from the sun (the same kind of rays that give you a sunburn). Without the ozone layer, the sun's rays

could be much more harmful. However, when produced at lower elevations in the atmosphere, ozone can be very harmful to human health. Pollution, especially from burning fossil fuels, leads to chemical reactions in the air that make ozone. In addition to being a health hazard (it causes serious breathing problems), it is also a greenhouse gas, trapping heat in the atmosphere. Ozone has a very short lifespan, from a few hours to a few weeks, but its strong ability to trap heat makes it a threat, especially in urban areas.

Nitrous Oxide, N_2O Nitrous oxide is a very potent greenhouse gas that usually comes from agriculture (farming) or land use change. It is made up of two nitrogen atoms and one oxygen atom. Nitrous oxide typically comes from nitrogen fertilizers being used on farms, but it can also be produced during industrial processes and burning fuel. As a greenhouse gas, nitrogen is about 237 times more powerful than carbon dioxide, although there is a lot less of it in the atmosphere. Nitrous oxide usually stays in the atmosphere for longer than 100 years, with the average being about 120 years. This means it lasts longer than methane, but not quite as long as carbon dioxide.

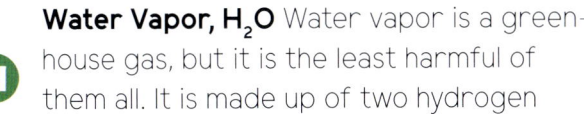**Water Vapor, H_2O** Water vapor is a greenhouse gas, but it is the least harmful of them all. It is made up of two hydrogen atoms and one oxygen atom. Water vapor sometimes counts as a greenhouse gas because it contributes to trapping heat from the sun. However, it has a shorter effect than the others, because water vapor more easily shifts into liquid water (rain) or solid forms such as ice or snow as part of the water cycle. Ultimately, it is in the atmosphere for around 10 days, which is not very long, before it changes into another form.

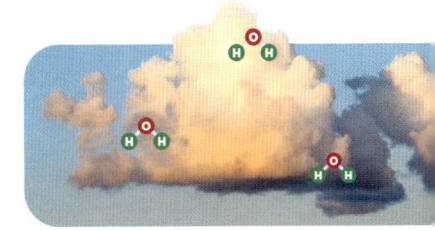

Even though there are five greenhouse gases, most people only refer to carbon dioxide. This is because carbon dioxide is the most common greenhouse gas in our atmosphere, and it accounts for about 80% of human-made greenhouse gas emissions. Because of this, you might see "CO_2 equivalent" as a measurement for emissions. Scientists will measure how strong each of the greenhouse gases is and then calculate it as if only carbon dioxide were causing it to make it simpler to talk about.

LINKING CARBON AND WARMING

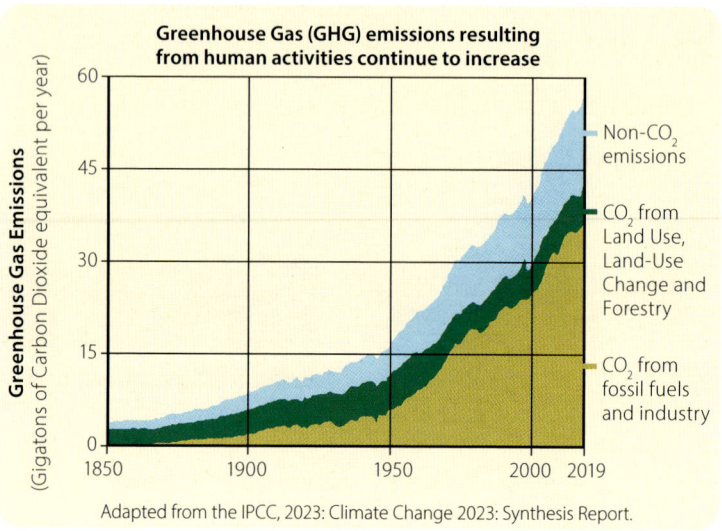

Adapted from the IPCC, 2023: Climate Change 2023: Synthesis Report.

This is a graph showing the increase in greenhouse gas emissions since 1850. These emissions were produced by people and not naturally occurring. You can see that it is still rising steeply.

Human beings have been on the planet for hundreds of thousands of years. Interestingly, we have only seen carbon in the atmosphere increase in the last few centuries.

Notice that in the graph above, there are no documented emissions from fossil fuels and industry until after 1850. Looking at a timeline of human invention over the past few hundred years, there are a few standout inventions that point us to how we got so much excess carbon in the atmosphere.

In 1859, the first oil well was drilled in Pennsylvania. This invention was soon followed by the first oil pipeline in 1862. Pipelines for oil and natural gas were not very efficient, however, until the late 1940s, when pipelines began to be built all over the country.

In 1886, the first gasoline-powered car was invented by Carl Benz (whose name lives on in Mercedes-Benz), and this triggered a wave of interest in "horseless carriages" as cars were known then. By making the assembly of his vehicles as efficient as possible (he helped improve the idea of an assembly line), Henry Ford made cars affordable, producing the Model A first in 1903, and introducing the famous Model T in 1908. The Model T was a very popular car as it was very affordable. This meant a lot of people were able to buy cars, and wanted good roads to drive them on, which meant cutting down forests and other natural habitats to build roads.

In 1903, the Wright Brothers first flew in a powered airplane. Incredibly, the first jet plane was introduced only a few decades later, in 1939. The invention and development of planes made travel much easier. When people traveled to new places, they also brought with them technologies enabled by fossil fuels, spreading this technology around the globe. This eventually also lead to the shipping of goods and products, meaning that large factories were able to build products for the whole planet, leading to more mining and pollution.

Keeping in mind these key technology dates that led to wider fossil fuel use and landscape change, let's look at the graph of greenhouse gases again.

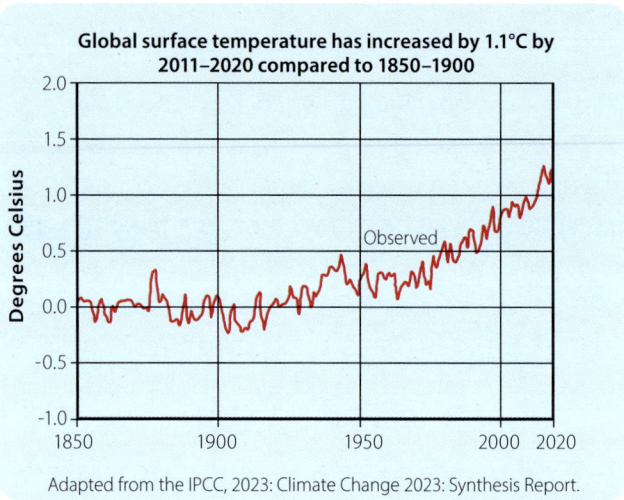

Adapted from the IPCC, 2023: Climate Change 2023: Synthesis Report.

This graph documents the global warming recorded since 1850. Notice how this graph also increases sharply on the right side.

These graphs show us that greenhouse gases have been emitted at a rising rate since 1850, and that global temperatures have been rising at a similar rate at the exact same time.

Scientists have proven (see page 43) that human beings are causing climate change, mostly through emitting greenhouse gases. In 2020, it was declared that the entire Earth had warmed more than 1.1 degrees Celsius (1.9 degrees Fahrenheit). This might not sound like a large number, but when it comes to climate, warming by even a few degrees means big changes for the planet.

CARBON SOURCES AND SINKS

Carbon emissions can also be taken back out of the atmosphere and stored. This is called **carbon sequestration** *(say it, see-quest-ray-shun)*, where emissions are removed from the atmosphere and held in a carbon sink, such as in the ocean or underground, where they can't contribute to the greenhouse effect.

Carbon sinks don't usually hold carbon forever, but it can stay in one place for a very long time, depending on which carbon sink it is in. Think of the sinks as train stations, where the carbon can stay and wait for the next carbon source to take them somewhere else. Usually, the cycle will take carbon throughout the different "spheres."

The lithosphere usually holds carbon for the longest time. In fact, the lithosphere contains 99% of all carbon on the planet! Most of the carbon in the lithosphere won't go into other carbon sinks, as it's deep within the Earth.

Although many carbon sources are human-made, the Earth also has naturally occurring carbon sources. One of those is decomposing plants. For example, when microbes and fungi break down an old tree, they release some of the carbon inside the tree back into the atmosphere.

Earth has many natural carbon sinks. Typically, forests are carbon sinks. As trees and plants photosynthesize (turn sunlight into energy sources), they draw carbon dioxide out of the atmosphere and store it in their trunks and roots. As part of the process of photosynthesis, plants produce oxygen. This is how forests are able to clean the air, by removing some carbon dioxide and turning it into oxygen.

NET-ZERO

So, if carbon emissions are heating the planet, what can we do?

The good news is that there are many ways to decrease the amount of greenhouse gas emissions. They range from using different energy sources to farming differently and adopting different forms of transportation. Taken together, these changes can make big impacts on how many greenhouse gases we release daily.

One of the most well-known goals for our emissions is getting them to net-zero. **Net-zero** means we emit the same amount of greenhouse gases at the same rate they are being stored, so there is no extra heating of the planet. This will prevent climate change from getting worse. Achieving net-zero is a difficult task, but it's possible. Strategies to achieve net-zero include maximizing the Earth's natural carbon sinks, like forests, and cutting our current rate of emission down significantly.

INDUSTRY GREENHOUSE EMISSIONS

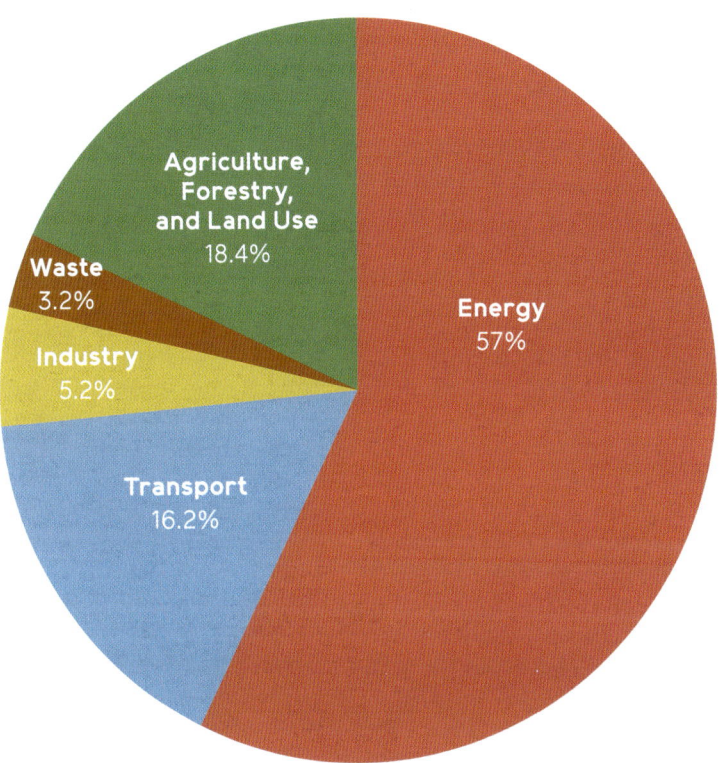

Before we can talk about cutting emissions, it's important to learn how and where we are emitting greenhouse gases.

One way to look at how humans are emitting greenhouse gases is this pie chart above showing emissions "by sector." By **sector** is a way to divide up sources of emissions based on how they were produced, so we can get a clearer picture of what is going on. In this graph, the main sectors shown are energy, industry, waste, transport, agriculture, forestry, and land use. But what do each of those mean?

Energy The largest slice includes energy that is used to create electricity for homes, factories, and businesses. We use a lot of energy in our lives globally, and, right now, most of that energy is created by burning fossil fuels.

Transport Transport includes the carbon released from driving cars, ships, and planes. Transportation across the world also burns fossil fuels, usually in the form of gasoline, diesel fuel, or other oil products. Burning gas emits carbon dioxide directly into the atmosphere.

Industry Industry is a smaller slice of global emissions, but significant when it comes to warming. Industry refers to companies that create or manufacture

materials that release carbon in the production process. For example, when cement is made, rocks are heated to very high temperatures, and this can release carbon that was trapped in the rocks.

Waste Waste is the smallest slice of the total emissions of greenhouse gases, but it is still a big problem. Today, we create a lot of waste, which we either burn or put in a landfill. When waste sits in landfills, it can start to release methane into the planet's atmosphere.

Agriculture, forestry, and land use Our use of land can also release greenhouse gases. Farming, or agriculture, can produce greenhouse gas emissions through fertilizers and poor soil health (breaking up soil releases stored carbon into the air). This sector also includes when people cut down or burn forests and other habitats to make room for something else. The greenhouse gases here are released when plants burn or decompose at rapid rates. Other emissions from agriculture come from livestock, such as cows burping methane.

Clearly, the world needs agriculture, industry, forestry, and transportation options. But there are changes we can make to make these sectors cleaner and healthier, with fewer greenhouse gas emissions.

Carbon Footprint

Another way to measure climate impact is through **carbon footprints**. A carbon footprint is a measurement of how much carbon a person (or group) emits. Carbon footprints can be measured personally or on a community level. You have carbon footprint, and you are also part of your neighborhood's carbon footprint, your city's carbon footprint, and your country's carbon footprint. Carbon footprints vary based on the

choices we make, such as the transportation we use, how much we throw away, what we eat, and so on.

GLOBAL CLIMATE EMISSIONS

Just as different sectors cause more emissions than others, some countries have caused more carbon emissions than others.

There are three ways to measure how a country produces greenhouse gases: by capita (per person), historical emissions, or yearly emissions.

Per capita emissions are emissions per person. Measuring emissions this way means dividing a country's emissions by the population. This is a way to try and measure each citizen's carbon footprint. Countries with more people usually have more emissions

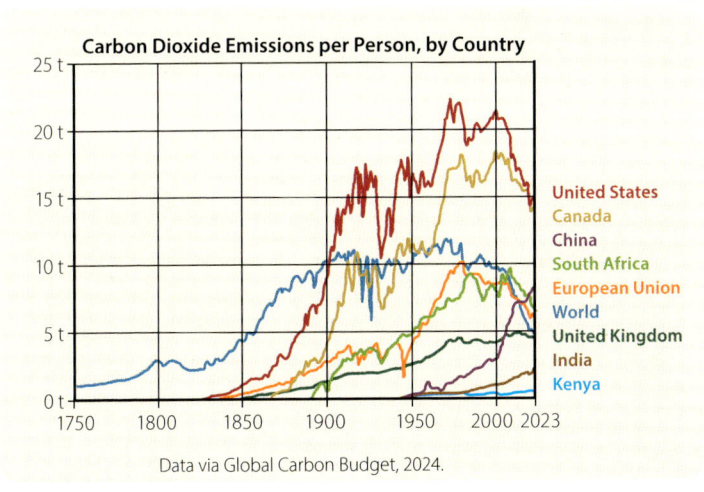

Data via Global Carbon Budget, 2024.

than countries with smaller populations, so measuring footprint this way tries to make countries easier to compare to each other.

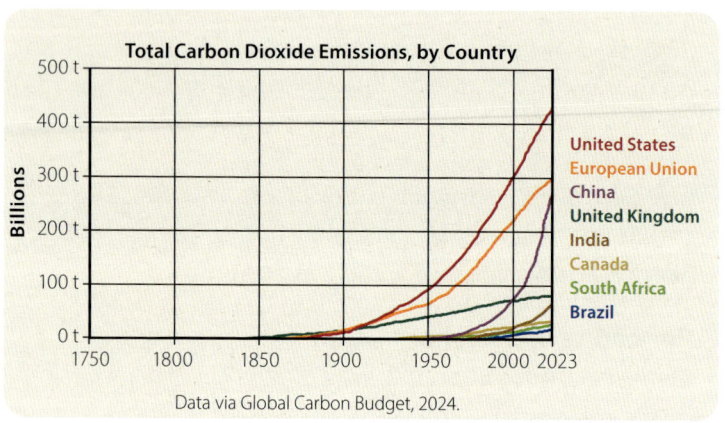

Data via Global Carbon Budget, 2024.

Historical emissions Historical emissions measure all the emissions a country has ever produced. This means that countries like England, which have burned coal in high amounts for longer than most other countries, would have more historical emissions. Historical emissions are harder to measure because we can only make educated guesses about the emissions of the past, but they put more responsibility on countries that have been emitting excess carbon for longer.

Yearly emissions Yearly emissions measure how many emissions countries produce per year. This is an up-to-date look at which countries are currently emitting the most.

These different ways of measuring emissions are used to try and answer an important question: Who is most responsible and needs to lower their carbon emissions first? Should a country that has not emitted a lot of carbon be responsible for cleaning it up?

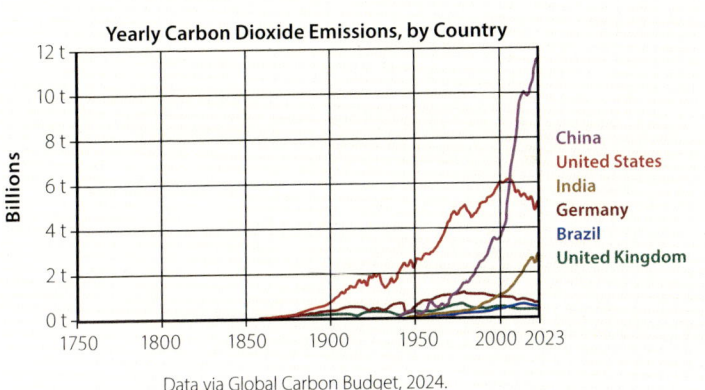

Data via Global Carbon Budget, 2024.

No matter which approach one uses to determine overall emissions, countries like the USA and China are always in the top 3 biggest emitters. This means these countries are responsible for producing a lot of greenhouse gas emissions, often more than many other countries put together. This also means to reach net-zero, these countries need to put in a lot of effort to fix their climate footprint.

How We Know

Scientists around the world have been studying climate change for decades, and we know that the world's climate today is different from what it was in

the 1970s. Scientists have proven that our current climate is different from what it was in the past. They have also proven that the climate is warming faster because of greenhouse gas emissions.

But you might be wondering, since greenhouse gases are invisible, how do we know who is emitting them, where they are coming from, and how much is really in the air?

ICE CORES

When water freezes, little pockets of air get trapped in the ice. These tiny little air bubbles can be trapped in ice for a very long time. Typically, the deeper the ice, the older the air in the bubbles. In the 1950s, scientists realized that the old air in the bubbles could be measured, since they still had the same gases as when they froze. To measure those gases, scientists use special drills to extract "cores," which they get

from ice in the Arctic and Antarctic. This lets them study the gases from the air from long ago, as far back as 2.7 million years ago! Knowing what the atmosphere looked like then, and how many greenhouse gases were present, can help us learn a lot about what's happening now.

SAMPLING THE ATMOSPHERE

To measure greenhouse gases today, scientists test the atmosphere. Scientists have been sampling the atmosphere for carbon dioxide regularly since the 1950s. This atmospheric sampling is the longest-running experiment on greenhouse gases. Using all the data since then, scientists have found a significant increase in greenhouse gases between the air of the 1950s and the air today.

One way scientists measure the chemical makeup of an air sample is called **spectroscopy** (say it, spek-trohs-koh-pee). Have you ever seen a glass prism that turns white light into a rainbow? Prisms work because they split visible white light into its component colors. Spectroscopy is a little like that. It's a technique that

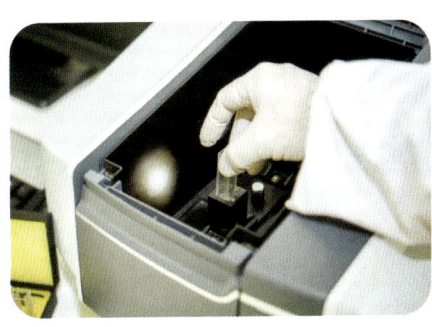

uses light to analyze the chemical makeup of matter. It involves shining a light source (or other radiation) and seeing which frequencies of light are absorbed or emitted. With spectroscopy, scientists can measure the gases in an air sample to see the amount of greenhouse gases and can note increases over time.

MEASURING OTHER PARTS OF THE EARTH

Scientists have documented the effects of climate change very well. Higher water levels indicate that there are higher levels of greenhouse gases in the atmosphere, and that they are causing heating. Melting ice at the poles, in the Arctic, and in Antarctica is causing rising ocean levels, and because water expands as it warms, ocean levels are rising further. Ocean acidity has also increased with higher greenhouse gas levels.

Scientists can measure all of these effects and have documented the rising sea levels, rising ocean acidity, and loss of polar ice. And you don't need to head to the Arctic to see this first-hand. Glacier National Park, in Montana, is named for its many glaciers, but over the past 50 years, many have shrunk, and they may be gone by the end of this century.

EFFECTS ON DIFFERENT SPECIES

Many species of plants, animals, and other creatures are also showing us that the climate is changing. Scientists have documented these changes as well. Some species, such as corals, are only able to live in very specific places that stay at specific temperatures. When their homes grow warmer and more unstable, these more delicate species start suffering, because they can no longer handle their environment.

The monarch butterfly has also been affected significantly by climate change. Monarchs rely on temperature to know when to migrate, but with warming temperatures, they aren't always migrating on time in the fall and winter, which leads to smaller numbers.

Other species in the world have adapted because the climate has been changing. For example, tawny owls in Europe are starting to become browner and less white. When there is less snow in the winter they no longer need white camouflage *(say it, cam-uh-flaj)* as much.

Are We the Problem?

Scientific research has made it clear that people's actions are the main cause of climate change. And that's not always easy to accept. After all, if climate change is our fault, you might wonder, are people bad for the planet?

While human actions have caused a lot of negative effects, humans are also capable of creating solutions. Human beings have lived on Earth for several hundred thousand years, and our actions have only led to global climate change in the last few centuries. Before this, human beings lived in relative harmony with the Earth, using the resources we needed, but not too much.

Therefore, it's not humanity that is the issue, but the choices that we collectively make. And if the problem is a matter of choices, that means we can make different choices that are better for the planet.

Climate Action Needs Everyone

Climate sciences are great because through them we can study the effects of a changing climate!

Meteorologists study the atmosphere and weather.

Geologists study the rocks and ground beneath our feet.

Hydrologists study water and the many ways it behaves.

Ecologists study how biomes and habitats survive and thrive.

Biologists study animals, plants, and other life forms.

These scientists and more have come together to compare their results so that we have a wider understanding of our Earth's systems.

Just as these scientists have come together to study the Earth and climate change, many other people are coming together to try and keep climate change from getting worse.

Engineers design machines and other solutions to create clean energy.

Lawyers and politicians figure out what rules to put in place so that we can work together to save the planet.

Teachers educate others about the risks and solutions to climate change.

Construction workers build the climate solutions we use to keep people safe.

Farmers work to feed our planet even as conditions get more difficult.

And regular people like **you** can help make change, come up with ideas and inventions, and make the world a better place. Many jobs can contribute to a healthier planet! Anyone can find their own unique way to work towards a clean and healthy future.

It's important to remember that none of us are alone in taking climate action. If you want to help and make a change, find the adults in your life who are already making a difference and ask how you can help.

Big Problems Require Big Solutions

Climate change affects so much of our lives. The more emissions increase, the more the climate will continue to change. Increased greenhouse gases in the atmosphere can lead to harsh impacts. We see proof every year that global warming is affecting us in negative ways. Storms have never been stronger than they are now, oceans are higher than they have been for centuries, and greenhouse gas levels are the highest they have ever been in human existence.

Thankfully, there are also a lot of solutions! And humans have already shown that we can cooperate to solve big problems: consider the ozone layer.

THE HOLE IN THE SKY: HOW WE HELPED THE OZONE LAYER

In 1985, scientists realized that there was a hole in what we call the ozone layer. The ozone layer is part of the Earth's upper atmosphere, and it protects life on Earth from the harshest parts of the sun's rays. The hole meant those harsh rays could get through to the surface of the Earth, and they would become dangerous for life.

The hole in the ozone layer was getting bigger because of chemicals that we were putting in the atmosphere. Those chemicals were called chlorofluorocarbons *(say it, chlor-o-flore-o-car-buns)*, or CFCs for short, and they were rising into the atmosphere and destroying the ozone layer. CFCs were in hairspray and refrigerators, and when humans used these products, we released these chemicals into the atmosphere.

Once humans saw the damage, we acted. Countries agreed to ban CFCs, and this greatly reduced their use. Companies turned away from using CFCs in their products. People looked for solutions and made their voices heard. The damaging CFCs have now been so significantly reduced that the ozone layer is healing itself. It should be fully healed within this century.

This is *huge*! Humans came together to solve a global problem that threatened us all: the hole in the ozone layer. This means we can come together to solve the climate crisis too.

A Field Guide to Climate Change Causes (and Solutions)

There are two field guides in this book. The first details the *causes* of climate change, how you can spot them in your daily life, and solutions to reduce those causes. The second details the *impacts* of climate change, how you can spot them, and how you can prepare for them.

Climate change is like a faucet over a bucket. The water (carbon) coming out of the faucet is flowing too fast, and the bucket (the atmosphere) is starting to overflow. The faucet being "on" represents a *cause* of climate change. Water spilling over the edge and onto the ground represents an *impact* of climate change.

To deal with climate change, we need to address the causes, but we also need to adapt to the effects we are already seeing. It is important to know how to see both causes and impacts to protect the people and the planet from the worst effects of climate change.

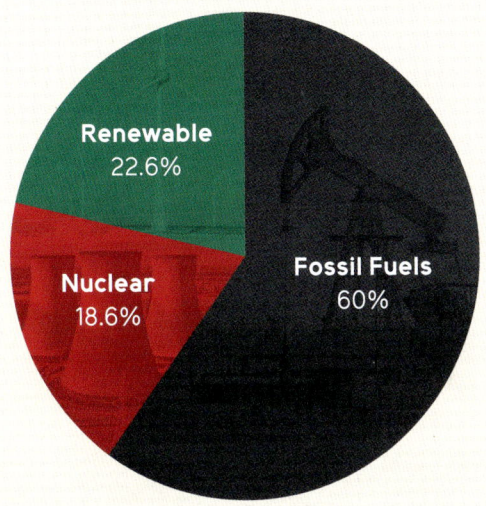

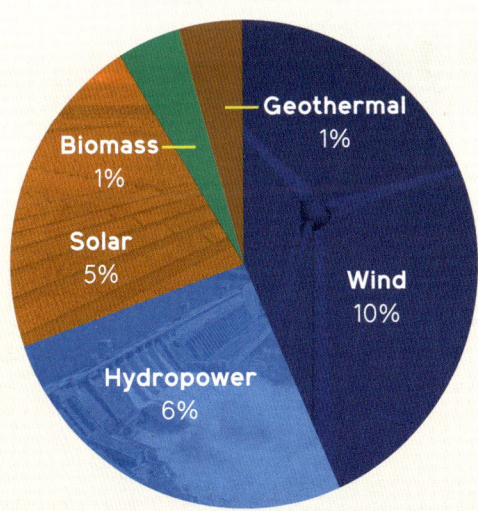

ENERGY SOURCES

We use energy to power our homes, schools, cars, and many other parts of our daily lives. We need energy and electricity, but historically, we have used sources of energy that are dirty and hurt the planet. The good news is that scientists have discovered many ways to produce energy that don't cause as much harm, and we are using them all over the world. Here is a field guide for all the kinds of energy we use in the world, which can be defined as renewable or non-renewable.

Non-Renewable Energy

Non-renewable energy comes from sources that are found in limited amounts on the planet. Once hey are gone, they are permanently used up. Most non-renewable energy sources are called fossil fuels. They are called fossil fuels because they are made of ancient lifeforms, like plants and plankton, that lived and died millions of years ago. These plants and other lifeforms were buried deep underground and slowly turned into the coal, oil, and gas that we mine out of the ground. Fossil fuels are non-renewable, which means we will run out of them if we keep using them, and they are also the biggest cause of climate change. To turn fossil fuels into energy, we burn them, which releases gases like carbon dioxide into the atmosphere.

Let's be clear, fossil fuels have been useful! They have helped us build the comfortable lives we have today. Because of fossil fuels, we have a world with cars, airplanes, computers, and more.

However, it's also true that our stable climate allowed for those same developments. Now that the climate is less stable, we will have to spend more time and energy protecting ourselves from floods, fires, diseases, and other climate impacts when we could be using that time for more useful things.

Coal

Coal is a fossil fuel that looks a lot like a black rock, and we have been burning it as fuel for thousands of years. Coal is one of the dirtiest fossil fuels, as it releases a lot of harmful chemicals into the air when it is burned. Air pollution from coal is dangerous to breathe, and it produces a lot of pollutants in the atmosphere. Even mining it is dangerous. Coal miners often get "black lung" from inhaling coal dust. Coal is the fossil fuel we use least often today, but it is still used to create electricity in many countries.

HOW MUCH DO WE USE?

Coal makes up around 16.7% of the yearly energy use in the US. This is the lowest it has ever been since we

started using coal, and this is because other energy sources are generally cleaner and more efficient than coal, so its use is dropping.

WHERE DOES IT COME FROM?

Coal comes from the ground, and people and machines mine it out. We have been mining coal for hundreds of years, so now, to reach coal, we often have to go much deeper than we used to.

BENEFITS

Coal is more efficient in electricity generation than burning wood. Coal is what first made traveling by train possible, and it kept a lot of people warm in the past. Coal use also powered many of the technological developments that led to our current modern technology.

PROBLEMS

Coal is an incredibly dirty fuel. Not only does it release a lot of carbon dioxide into the atmosphere, but it also releases a lot of other chemicals when it is burned. These chemicals can cause acid rain, which is very damaging to the environment. They can also cause respiratory illnesses in people, making it harder to breathe. Also, mining coal is very dangerous, and people have been injured or gotten sick from working in coal mines.

Oil

HOW MUCH DO WE USE?
The USA uses oil to power less than 1% of its electricity mix. But that doesn't mean we don't use much oil at all. Oil is also used to make different products, some of which go to our cars and planes as fuel, and some of which go to different products like plastic, pesticides, and many others. Oil is used to make gasoline and other fuels, which make up about 36 percent of the overall US energy supply.

WHERE DOES IT COME FROM?
Oil is found underground where oceans used to be located centuries ago. Tiny organisms in the ocean died and fell to the bottom, where they were slowly transformed into oil by heat and pressure. Getting oil out of the ground is difficult: Wells have to be drilled, and the oil has to be pumped up to the surface. Some reservoirs are found underwater, so there are oil rigs in the middle of the ocean pumping oil up from inside the sea floor.

Like coal and gas, it took millions of years for oil to form underground, so we are currently unable to make more of it, making it non-renewable.

BENEFITS
Oil is more efficient than burning coal in many ways. It is easier to transport across countries and oceans, and it pollutes less per pound than coal does.

PROBLEMS

Oil is a major polluter, and burning oil for fuel is one of the leading drivers of climate change.

Oil spills are a serious problem as well, and they happen somewhat often. Oil spills occur when oil rigs, pipelines, or tanker ships carrying oil are damaged and spill oil into the environment. When oil spills out, wildlife is harmed and sometimes killed, and it contaminates freshwater, potentially harming further living things.

Gas

HOW MUCH DO WE USE?

The USA generates 42% of all its energy from natural gas. This is the largest energy source America uses. We use gas not only to generate energy, but also to heat and cook in our homes.

WHERE DOES IT COME FROM?

Natural gas, like the other fossil fuels, has formed over long periods of time, and gas is usually found near oil deposits. Natural gas pockets underground contain varying levels of gas. If a pocket is found close to the Earth's surface, then it has some gas in it, but not a lot. If a pocket is found deep underground, there is usually a lot more gas in it.

There is a subset of natural gas called **biogas**, which is a type of gas that is created by decomposing matter. This occurs near landfills and other places where waste is kept.

BENEFITS

Gas is known as the "cleanest" fossil fuel because it doesn't release as many harmful chemicals as coal or oil when burned to make energy.

Using biogas coming from landfills or waste collection sites provides an opportunity to generate energy while also getting rid of some methane emissions from the landfills.

PROBLEMS

Even if it is the "cleanest" fossil fuel, it still contributes heavily to our emissions of greenhouse gases. Not only does burning gas release lots of carbon dioxide, but when there is a gas leak, it is released as methane. Remember, methane is more effective in the short term compared to CO_2 at heating the planet.

Natural gas leaks can also be very dangerous if they happen in someone's home (explosions can result), and using natural gas to cook indoors can cause health problems, like carbon monoxide poisoning.

Nuclear

Nuclear energy is non-renewable, but it is not a fossil fuel like coal, gas, or oil. Scientists use uranium *(say it, yur-ay-nee-um)*, a radioactive element, and split its atoms to create a lot of heat and energy. This then turns water into steam, which rotates turbines to create electricity. However, uranium is rare on Earth, and it must be mined, so it is considered non-renewable.

HOW MUCH DO WE USE?

The United States uses nuclear energy to generate 18% of our electricity, which is a little more than the amount of electricity we make from coal. Around the world, some countries don't use nuclear energy at all, and some countries use it a whole lot. France uses nuclear energy to generate 64% of its energy!

WHERE DOES IT COME FROM?

Nuclear energy comes from large buildings called nuclear power plants. In nuclear power plants, scientists break atoms of one larger element into atoms of two smaller elements. This process generates a lot of heat and helps produce steam, which then makes electricity.

BENEFITS

Using nuclear energy is much cleaner than using fossil fuels and doesn't hurt people's health as much as fossil fuels.

PROBLEMS

Nuclear power plants can use up a lot of water when generating electricity. Accidents at nuclear power plants can also be very dangerous. Scientists spend a lot of time making sure nuclear accidents don't happen, and accidents are very rare compared to those on oil rigs or in coal mines. Since nuclear accidents can cause long-lasting damage, they can be very scary, making people afraid of nuclear power. Nuclear power also creates nuclear waste, which is dangerous and needs to be carefully stored for a very long time.

Solutions: Renewable Energy

Many sources of energy are **renewable energy** sources, or sources that will not run out. Nature provides these sources, and they don't have the same health and safety problems as fossil fuels. Most renewable energy sources don't require us to burn anything to produce them, so they don't release excess carbon into the atmosphere. Renewable energy sources also pollute much less, which means they are safe for people to be around, and they don't cause health problems.

We are using more and more renewable sources of energy every day, which is good news for the planet and for our health. But we'll need a lot more renewable energy if we are going to stop emitting

greenhouse gases. Right now, the USA only uses renewable sources of energy for 22.6% of its energy generation. Even though that is a small amount of our current energy sources, we know that people are starting to turn to renewable energy across the country and around the world.

However, renewable energy can have limits too, and you'll find that many renewable sources of energy need to be in specific places to work well. This can make using renewable energy a little harder, but when we use many renewable sources of energy together, we can solve those problems.

Solar Energy

Solar energy is made using the light and heat from the sun's rays. Devices called **solar panels** catch the sun's rays and turn them into electricity. Solar panels create clean energy that can be used in a variety of ways, and people are installing more solar panels every day.

HOW MUCH DO WE USE?

Solar energy makes up almost 5% of all our energy and about 24% of all the renewable energy the USA uses. Solar energy is growing very quickly, though, and so the percentage is likely to go up soon.

WHERE DOES IT COME FROM?

The sun! When the sun's light hits a solar panel, energy is produced. The panels are made of a special silicone glass and metals. A solar panel can make energy for around 30 years until it needs to be recycled.

BENEFITS

Unlike fossil fuels, solar energy doesn't pollute when it makes electricity. It is harnessing the same energy that plants use to grow. Solar panels can be deployed in many ways. They can go on the rooftops of homes to power small areas, or in large fields to generate as much electricity as possible. These large fields are often called solar farms.

Solar panels also make it easy to create power in faraway places. If someone in a hard-to-get-to area wanted a streetlamp, it could be a difficult process connecting them to a power grid. Solar panels are great for energy production in hard-to-reach areas, because electricity can be generated without needing to connect to a power plant.

PROBLEMS

Solar energy uses the energy from the sun, which has been shining for billions of years. However, sometimes it's cloudy, and the sun sets each day. Solar panels only work when it's daytime and there are clear skies. In the same way, solar panels don't work very well where there are lots of trees above to provide shade.

This means that solar panels aren't ideal everywhere. Some areas, such as the Pacific Northwest, where it's typically cloudy and rainy, aren't a great fit, as they won't make a lot of energy there.

Because energy generation through solar panels is limited, we have turned to **battery storage**. Large batteries can store the energy created by solar panels when it is sunny, and store it until it is needed later, even when solar panels aren't making electricity.

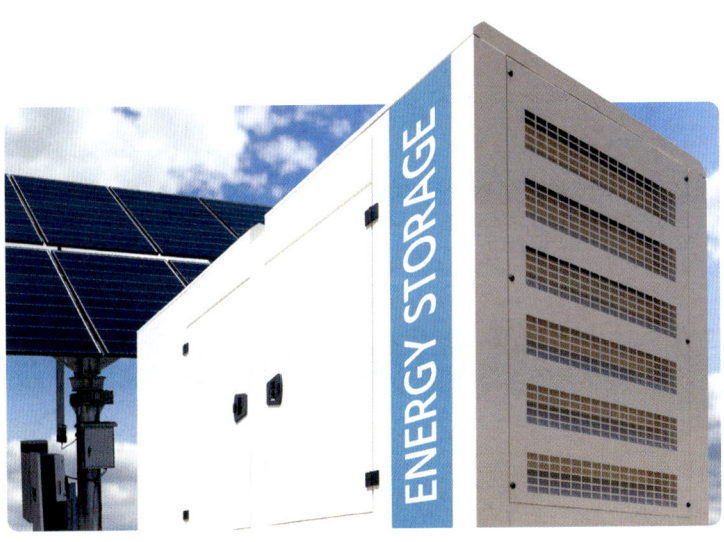

Wind Energy

Wind energy is made by catching the wind. Usually, wind energy is harvested through **wind turbines**, which are giant machines that look like fans or pinwheels. Wind turbines make electricity when the wind spins their blades and turns a generator inside. Wind energy is clean and can generate a lot of energy in windy areas, but it isn't very helpful in places with only a little wind.

HOW MUCH DO WE USE?

Wind energy makes up almost 10% of the USA's power supply, and 45% of all the renewables the USA uses. This makes it the largest single source of renewable energy in the USA.

WHERE DOES IT COME FROM?

Wind is caused by uneven heating on the Earth. When the sun rises and hits a beach and the nearby ocean, for example, the two areas heat differently. Land warms up faster than water, and the uneven temperatures between the two create wind. Wind is sometimes unpredictable, and part of why the weather shifts between temperatures, but some winds are very predictable throughout the day, and those places are where we put wind turbines.

When the wind blows near a turbine, the giant blades are pushed. This movement powers a generator, which produces electricity, which is then carried elsewhere through cables.

Wind farms, where we harvest wind energy, can come in two general types. The first is on land, where wind turbines are secured on the ground. The second are offshore wind farms, where turbines are concentrated in the ocean. Some offshore wind turbines are secured onto the sea floor, and others are floating, secured by anchors.

BENEFITS

Humans have been harnessing the power of the wind since they invented sailboats. Windmills have been made for thousands of years to pump water and to grind grains into flour.

Wind energy is a clean and safe source of electricity. Wind energy has grown very quickly in the USA.

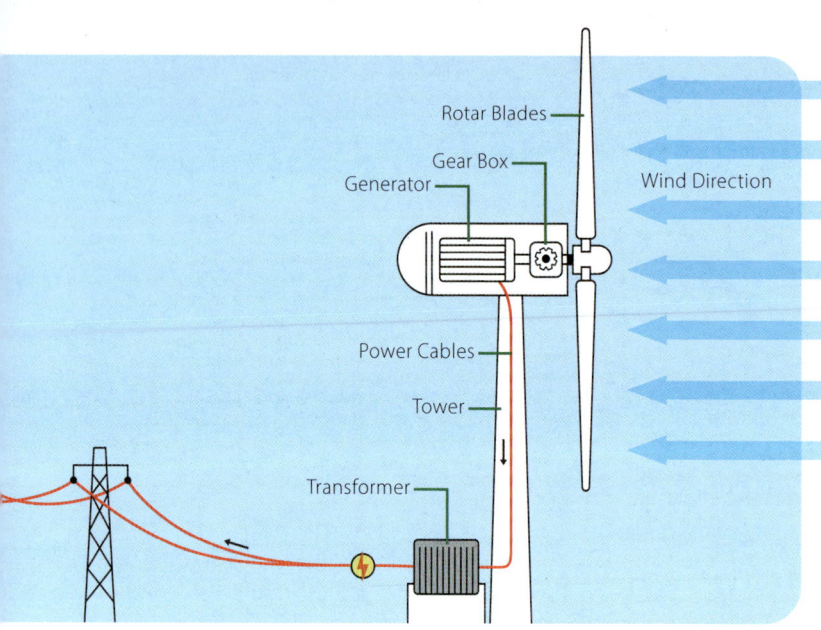

It made up less than 1% of the country's electricity in 1990. Since then, we have discovered many ways to make wind turbines more efficient and generate more electricity.

PROBLEMS

The wind isn't always blowing! This means wind farms also use battery storage, just like solar power, to store excess energy.

Wind turbines' blades can sometimes harm wildlife, including birds. Thankfully, this problem has many solutions. By painting wind turbine blades a color that isn't white, even just one blade on each turbine, birds can avoid running into the blades and getting hurt. Critics of clean energy like to use this potential harm as a reason not to install wind power, but they often ignore how many birds will be harmed by climate change if we continue to burn fossil fuels instead.

Hydropower

Hydropower uses the motion of flowing water to make electricity. Hydropower usually comes from structures called **dams**, which use flowing river water to spin turbines that generate electricity. As long as rivers keep flowing, hydropower is possible.

HOW MUCH DO WE USE?
In the United States, hydropower produces 6% of the energy we use and 28% of all the renewable energy made in the USA.

WHERE DOES IT COME FROM?

Hydropower is sourced from flowing rivers. Humans have been building ways to harness the power of water for thousands of years, like using water wheels. But now, we use hydropower to produce electricity. The first dams built to generate electricity were constructed in the 1880s, and we have been using them ever since.

BENEFITS

Hydropower has been used for a long time. The energy that comes from hydropower is clean and doesn't release carbon into the atmosphere. We can also get more energy out of our current dams by upgrading the technology used, which creates more energy for the same amount of water.

PROBLEMS

Dams often damage or change river habitats. So while they produce clean, renewable energy, they can damage biodiversity. Also, dams need to be large for energy production to be worthwhile, and large dams also create reservoirs (human-made lakes) that flood large areas of land. Humans have built pretty much all the dams that make sense to build all over the world. Dams are a large source of clean energy, but hydropower is unlikely to grow.

Geothermal Energy

Geothermal energy is energy created using heat that comes from deep in the Earth. Far beneath the ground under our feet, there are areas with very hot water and steam, and we can use that steam to make electricity and heat our homes. While geothermal energy is renewable, it's not available everywhere, as the underlying rocks must be formed just right for it to be possible.

HOW MUCH DO WE USE?

Compared to other sources of renewable energy, we do not use a lot of geothermal to create electricity. Geothermal electricity only makes up less than 1% of our electricity, and 2% of renewable-generated electricity. This is not only because geothermal relies on specific locations, but also because geothermal energy isn't always used to generate electricity. It's often used for direct heating instead.

WHERE DOES IT COME FROM?

Most places where geothermal is active on Earth occur around the edges of tectonic plates, or near larger cracks that allow the heat from below the Earth to penetrate the upper layers. There are also areas of underground geothermal energy, which can be drilled down to and brought to the surface.

In the USA, most available geothermal exists in the Western part of the country, and that is where most American geothermal power plants can be found. Geothermal is used outside of power plants in other parts of America as well, but not as often.

BENEFITS

Unlike other sources of clean energy, geothermal energy doesn't just get used in a power plant. Humans also use geothermal as a source of heat and use it directly to heat homes and other buildings without turning it into electricity first.

And because it does not use fossil fuels, geothermal energy releases very few emissions. Some naturally occurring carbon dioxide emissions come from areas of geothermal activity, but they are small compared to fossil fuel emissions.

PROBLEMS

Geothermal energy works best in areas where it's easy to access the steam or heated water. That means, if some areas are covered in hundreds of feet of rock, you'd have to have to dig down very deep to reach it, which wouldn't always be worth it.

Biomass

Biomass is another word for burning wood or plant parts to make energy. Burning wood to make a campfire is an example of using biomass. Biomass is one of the oldest forms of energy use, and people all over the world still burn wood, dried stalks, and other biomass to heat their homes or cook food.

HOW MUCH DO WE USE?

Today, the USA uses biomass to generate less than 1% of its electricity and makes up 1% of its total renewables. Biomass used to be the most common energy source in America for centuries! People would burn wood and other plant matter to heat their homes, cook, and see in the dark. In the mid-1800s, however, coal became more popular, and since then, other fossil fuels have become more prominent.

WHERE DOES IT COME FROM?

Biomass comes from the biosphere—that is, living things! Biomass could be sticks that fell off a tree, or dried corn stalks after the corn has been harvested.

BENEFITS

Many of the biofuels burned for energy come from waste from other activities, like farming. This means that burning biomass for fuel also cuts down on waste.

When used responsibly, biomass is a safe way to generate small amounts of power. It can also be done on a small scale. For people who need to heat their homes or cook on fires, biomass is an accessible and simple way to generate energy.

PROBLEMS

Biomass is a renewable source of energy, but it replenishes itself more slowly than other forms of renewable energy. It takes a whole season, or even years, for biomass to grow to the point where it makes sense to burn it for fuel. This means we can run out of it if we use it too quickly.

Burning biomass to generate electricity also releases carbon dioxide and other pollutants into the atmosphere. It can also lead to negative health effects, like respiratory issues. This means that, while biomass is renewable, it isn't always the cleanest choice for energy production. Remember, though, burning biomass pollutes less than burning fossil fuels.

How we currently make and use energy is a big reason the Earth's climate is out of balance. But it's not the only reason. Let's look at some of the other causes of the carbon imbalance in the atmosphere.

Destruction of Nature

The second-biggest cause of the carbon imbalance in the atmosphere is the destruction of nature. This mostly happens in three ways: agriculture, forestry, and land use change. How do these things hurt the planet?

Agriculture

All the meals you ate today came from agriculture. **Agriculture** is a big word that means farming, and it can include growing crops and raising animals for food and other resources.

Farming is important, as it helps cities and towns grow and provides us with food. But the way we farm can release greenhouse gases into the atmosphere and damage our ecosystems.

One of the main harmful ways that our farming can hurt the planet is through monoculture farming.

Monoculture farming is a practice of farming where the farmer only grows one or two kinds of crops on the land year after year. They are usually planted in rows, covering large fields. This is not how plants usually grow in nature. Plants in nature usually grow alongside dozens of other plants.

Because monoculture farming isn't how plants naturally grow, farmers must buy fertilizers and pesticides to keep their crops healthy. However, pesticides and fertilizers are often made from fossil fuels, emit greenhouse gases, and can pollute our water. For example, fertilizer is the main source of the greenhouse gas nitrogen oxide.

Monoculture farming can also remove the greenhouse gases that are stored in the soil. When lots of different plants live mixed together, they help keep the soil full of nutrients that help other plants grow. When the soil is nutrient-dense like this, the top layer of soil, called topsoil, stores some greenhouse gases, keeping them out of the atmosphere. In a monoculture, plants remove nutrients from the soil without replacing them. This can lead to lower-quality soil. And when soil is made worse through monoculture farming, it starts to release that carbon back out into the atmosphere.

Forestry

Forests are the lungs of the Earth. In forests, photosynthesis happens on a huge scale, and large amounts of carbon dioxide in the atmosphere are converted into oxygen.

And when trees take in carbon dioxide and turn it into oxygen, they store the carbon inside themselves, removing it from the atmosphere. Look at this equation here:

$$6CO_2 + 6H_2O \xrightarrow{LIGHT} C_6H_{12}O_6 + 6O_2$$

Carbon dioxide + Water → Sugar + Oxygen

Trees and other plants use sunlight, carbon dioxide, and water to produce sugar and oxygen! Trees store the resulting carbon in their big trunks and roots. You might be wondering, how are forests a source of carbon emissions? They should be a carbon sink!

Forests usually *are* carbon sinks. Without forests, the carbon emissions from human actions would be much higher. But that's only true if the forests stay standing.

When humans cut down or burn forests, the trees that either decompose (break down) or burn release the carbon back out into the atmosphere. When humans start destroying forests to make room for development (cities, houses) or agriculture, all the carbon the trees were holding onto re-enters the atmosphere. Right now, humans are cutting down trees at such a fast rate that we're adding lots of carbon to the atmosphere.

Land-Use Change

Land-use change is when humans change natural landscapes. This means changing land from a forest

into a farm, turning a prairie into a suburban neighborhood, or a marsh into a city. Typically, we think of land use change in the way of destroying a natural ecosystem, or destroying nature, to make something that mostly benefits humans and ignores other creatures.

Land-use change can be positive or negative for the climate, but it is also the second largest cause of emissions in the world, so what does it mean?

To spot land use change, look around at where you are while reading this book. Maybe you are in a school or a house, which would be a building in a neighborhood. Maybe you're in a car or on a train, which is traveling on a highway or on tracks. It's likely that where you will sleep tonight is in a place where the land has been changed. Long ago, where you are could have been a forest, a prairie, a bog, or a marsh.

Solutions: Working with Nature

Destruction of nature usually occurs when humans change natural environments into something else. Thankfully, when it comes to changing how we use the land, there are solutions to keep emissions out of the atmosphere. Let's look at those next.

Some land-use change is positive for the planet's health. The Great Green Wall in Africa is an example of land-use change that is meant to protect the soil and create habitat. South of the Sahara Desert, climate change and over-farming were causing farmland to degrade or lose its ability to grow food. To address this, 11 countries are planting trees in one long wall. This will help regenerate *(say it, ree-JEN-er-ate)* the soil and increase biodiversity *(say it, bye-oh-dye-VER-sit-ee)*. The planned Wall is 8,000 kilometers long, or almost 5,000 miles long! So far, it's about 30% complete.

This is just one example of a solution of people coming together to work with nature, not against it. Many of the countries involved in the Green Wall are also planting trees that produce fruits or other foods, which means that they can still farm and get food, without sacrificing the soil's quality.

Compost Composting is a solution to poor soil that helps keep carbon in soil, reduces fossil-fuel-based fertilizers on farms, and reduces food waste. When food waste is put in a landfill, it creates methane emissions. However, when food waste and other plant matter are composted and allowed to break down slowly over time (often with the help of bacteria and insects), it secures carbon. The resulting compost can be used as an alternative to fertilizer.

Composting can be done in someone's backyard or for a whole city. Many cities are starting to include programs that collect compost from houses just like trash and recycling. Not only is it beneficial for farmers and the soil, but it also helps keep pests away from houses. While not everyone in the country has access to a composting program run by a city, it is becoming much more popular. And it helps the planet!

Industrial Emissions and Damage

"Industry" is what happens when we make things in factories. The items and materials we use every day are made by industry. Looking at a simple spiral-bound notebook, the plastic cover, the paper pages, and the metal spine are all made by different industries. Many kinds of industry, like making products out of metal, require a lot of heat. Heat generation causes a lot of emissions.

In industry, most of the emissions come from fossil fuels. These fossil fuels are used to power the factories, but a small amount, around one-third of industry's emissions, comes from the materials being made.

As an example, making cement produces many greenhouse gases. To make the base for cement, we heat limestone to a high temperature to cause chemical reactions. When limestone is heated this much, it releases carbon dioxide.

Solutions: Technology and Using Less

As technology improves, we are discovering ways to use better energy sources to power industry. We are also inventing new ways to make materials that use less energy, which prevents emissions from going into the atmosphere. Engineers and other scientists are working very hard on ways to make industry better for the environment.

Reusing the resources we already have is another way to decrease greenhouse gas emissions. If we recycle our metals, like aluminum, then we don't have

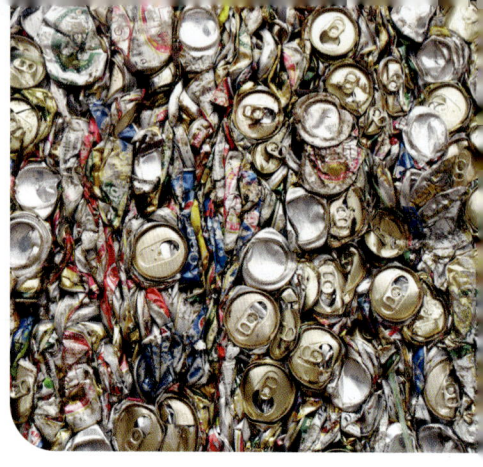

to damage habitats to make bigger aluminum mines and use lots of energy to process that aluminum. Instead, we melt the old aluminum and reuse it, which uses a lot less energy and releases fewer greenhouse gases.

Also, the more we can reuse the things we already have, then we don't need to make as many new things. This means we don't need to make as many materials and products, which makes the footprint of industry even lighter.

Transportation

Humans have invented many ways of moving around: bikes, boats, cars, trains, planes, and buses help keep people moving, get to work or the grocery store, and see their loved ones.

Currently, a lot of forms of transportation rely on fossil fuels. Vehicles like cars and planes burn fossil fuels to generate the power it takes to move. Transportation in the US produces more than 16% of the country's emissions, which is a lot.

Vehicles that burn fossil fuels don't just hurt the climate—they also hurt us. When vehicles burn fossil fuels, they release aerosols *(say it, air-oh-sols)*, little particles that stay in the air. These particles are bad for our health. When we breathe in aerosols, they can make our lungs and hearts less healthy.

Solutions: Effective Design and Electric Tech

Electric vehicles are a solution to vehicles that burn fossil fuels. These vehicles are charged with electricity and move without burning gas or oil. Electric vehicles don't release aerosols that hurt our health. But we also know that, to make electricity, we burn fossil fuels, so are they really better?

Electric vehicles become cleaner as our electricity sources become cleaner. Even if an area uses only 30% renewable energy in its energy mix, an electric car is running on clean energy 30% of its charge, while a gas-powered car is still running off 100% fossil fuels.

Vehicles like bikes and skateboards are great because they don't use energy at all except for the energy that humans provide. But bikes and skateboards can't move a lot of people at once, and not everyone can travel this way.

The best way to reduce greenhouse gases from transportation is to give large populations a lot of varied methods of transportation, including access to trains, buses, cars, and safe, easy ways to walk (especially in cities). Many places in America are designed for cars to get people everywhere. In some neighborhoods, people cannot safely walk to their grocery store or their friends' and family's houses. By designing and building areas where walking and biking are safe, cars and buses are electric, and trains can get people beyond their neighborhood, greenhouse gases will be reduced. These areas can make people less reliant on fossil fuel-burning transportation to get somewhere.

Waste

Think of a full trash can that you might see on the street, in your school, or at home. Now think of how much waste there is for your whole block, your neighborhood, your city. It's a lot of waste. What do we do with it all?

Waste is harmful to the planet in two ways. First, the ways we dispose of (get rid of) waste can release greenhouse gas emissions into the atmosphere. Overall, waste is responsible for 3.2% of our greenhouse gas emissions. Second, waste can damage the ecosystems around us.

To get rid of waste, we usually do two things. First, we send garbage to landfills. Landfills are big holes in the ground where we put trash. When the waste starts decomposing in the landfill, greenhouse gases, especially methane, are released into the atmosphere. This is a large source of emissions in the USA.

Waste can also be incinerated *(say it, in-sin-er-ay-ted)* or burned. This releases emissions into the atmosphere, as well as other dangerous aerosols that can hurt our health and the health of the environment around us.

Inspired by: *A Comprehensive Review of Atmospheric Air Pollutants Assessment Around Landfill Sites*, Salami and Popoola.

When we don't get rid of waste or litter and let it pile up, it can damage ecosystems. For example, animals can eat plastic by accident and choke, or they can get trapped by plastic waste. If there's too much litter in one place, life can't thrive, leading to habitat loss.

Solutions: Using Less, Reusing More, and the Circular Economy

One great way to reduce waste is called a **circular economy**. Right now, however, our economy is largely linear (or like a line).

Take a look at this diagram of using something in a linear way.

Whatever materials and work went into making the product in the first place just end up in a landfill. This not only wastes the limited materials we have (such as metals), but landfills are also a source of greenhouse gas emissions and take up a lot of space.

Now, look at this diagram of a circular economy.

A circular economy helps us make the most of our limited resources. In a linear economy, products are made, sold, used only once, and then thrown away. In a circular economy, the materials that go into products are reused or repurposed. This means that we don't have to use energy to mine for more materials or produce more at a factory. This helps protect the planet.

You've probably heard of the phrase "reduce, reuse, recycle." This reminds us of the best ways to keep waste out of landfills. But the order of that phrase matters. It's important to *reduce* what you and your community buy first, making sure you only buy what you need. After that, try to *reuse* what you already have to meet other needs. *Recycling* is the last step. It involves taking waste and turning it into new materials.

All of these steps will help keep trash out of landfills and lead to fewer emissions and less pollution in habitats. Thinking about how we create waste is a good way to show that you care about the world around us.

Climate Impacts (and Solutions)

The more we can stop emissions from happening, the better the future will be. But what about the emissions that are already in the atmosphere?

The emissions already in the atmosphere are very high. While trees can take greenhouse gases out of the atmosphere and shift them into the biosphere and lithosphere, it is a slow process, and much slower than the speed at which we are creating emissions. The current imbalance in the atmosphere leads to climate change impacts.

An **impact** of climate change is an effect of the climate changing. It is a result of the high amount of emissions that are already in the atmosphere.

The second part of this field guide will teach you how to spot the impacts of climate change. These are just as important as the causes, especially when it comes to protecting your community.

Not everywhere experiences the same impacts of climate change. A house on the coast of Maine is going to experience different impacts than an apartment in Arizona. The impacts, while different, can be just as serious, and it is important to know that while people may be dealing with different impacts, they all come from the same place: climate change.

WILD WEATHER

Perhaps the most well-known impact of climate change on our lives is changes in the weather. **Severe weather** is weather that can cause harm to people and other life. Severe weather has always existed, even before human-caused climate change. However, climate change causes more frequent and more intense storms. So, while the existence of severe weather is not due to climate change, climate change strengthens it and increases how often it happens. Climate change can even produce types of severe weather in places where that weather doesn't usually occur (heat waves in colder places, for example). These are the most common ways we see climate change in the weather, as well as ways to protect ourselves during them.

Heatwaves A heatwave is a period of unusually hot weather that lasts at least two days or longer. "Unusually hot" means that it is not typical of the local climate at that time of year. This means that it is hotter than historical averages for that area. Plants and animals can suffer greatly under extreme heat that they are not used to, and water can sometimes become scarce.

Heatwaves are becoming more frequent in the USA. Recently, in June 2025, the East Coast and New England areas
suffered from a heat wave that brought very hot temperatures that are rare for so early in the summer. In International Falls, Minnesota, in May 2025, a heat wave brought temperatures of 96 degrees to an area that is very far north and doesn't usually see those temperatures. The most intense heatwave in US history was in July 1936, which is very long ago. There are still a lot of heatwave records that have not been surpassed since then!

> **SAFETY DURING HEATWAVES** Find ways to cool off as much as possible. This means staying hydrated, finding shade, seeking places with air conditioning, or finding ways to stay wet, like pools or sprinklers.

Droughts A drought is a period of unusually low rain or snow. This means there is less rain and water, causing areas to become drier. This dryness can lead to hazards like fires or make it harder to grow food on farms. Droughts can last as little as a few weeks or as long as several years. Droughts and heatwaves can sometimes happen at the same time, making water hard to find when it is needed most.

In the western United States, there is still a severe megadrought. A megadrought means that a drought has lasted around 20 years. This megadrought started in 2000 and is still ongoing today. There have been some improvements in the rainfall of the area, but it has not improved enough to be back at the levels it was before the drought.

SAFETY DURING DROUGHTS Depending on the severity of droughts, water might be limited, so use water wisely and don't water lawns. During a drought, wildfires often occur, so avoid activities that can cause sparks.

Floods Floods occur when water builds up on land that is normally dry. Flooding can drown and displace many creatures, and because moving water is very powerful, it can even carry cars and houses over great distances. Flash floods are particularly dangerous, as they are incredibly speedy and can sometimes come faster than an evacuation warning.

In Texas, in July 2025, severe flooding affected the areas around the Guadalupe River. Heavy rains caused the river to flood beyond its normal banks, and many people were swept away. This was an instance of flash flooding that took people by surprise and ended tragically.

> **SAFETY DURING FLOODS** If a flood is slow, then professionals can predict it. Evacuation is very important. Look at flood maps, available online, to see if your neighborhood is vulnerable to flash floods and create a safety plan if you are.

Hurricanes Hurricanes are very powerful storms that form over water, and then move long distances, even going over land. Hurricanes are rotating systems of organized clouds and thunderstorms, and cause high winds, heavy rain, and flooding (especially "storm surges," a rapid rise in water level caused by a storm). Hurricanes form over warm water and grow stronger when the ocean is warm, so they are more common during summer months, but the warmer the oceans get, the more likely hurricanes out of season become. Hurricanes typically hit land near coasts, so if you live near a coast, it is important to know what to do during a hurricane.

In September 2024, Hurricane Helene grew quickly over the warm waters of the Gulf and hit the coasts of Florida. Helene had a lot of power; however, due to the moisture and energy it got from the warm Gulf, the storm traveled 100 miles north to hit the South Appalachian region, including North Carolina and Tennessee. Scientists have found that Helene was more powerful due to climate change, but the storm itself, like all storms, was a natural occurrence.

SAFETY DURING HURRICANES Obey evacuation orders when they are given for your area by professionals. The safest way to survive a hurricane is not to be there when one hits. Make an emergency kit, or bag ready to go, and have a family safety plan for hurricanes.

Tornadoes A tornado is a narrow column of air that is rapidly spinning, and they form in severe thunderstorms. Tornadoes can be very violent, growing from strong winds spinning around each other and can cause a lot of damage to homes and buildings, especially if the funnel cloud "touches down" on the ground.

In December 2021, a deadly tornado hit Kentucky, Illinois, Tennessee, Missouri, and Arkansas, causing a lot of damage and hurting a lot of people. Tornadoes aren't as influenced by climate change as other storms, but there is some evidence to suggest that climate change has created more favorable conditions in areas for tornadoes that don't usually see them.

SAFETY DURING TORNADOES Monitor weather alerts for tornado warnings and watches. Get to a safe part of your basement away from windows. If you do not have a basement, note where your closest safety shelter is for tornadoes.

Hailstorms Hailstorms occur when large particles of ice form inside thunderstorm clouds. Hail forms when rain is pulled upwards on updrafts, gathers together, and freezes at high altitudes. Eventually, hail becomes too heavy and falls to Earth. Hail can damage property, and large hail can be very dangerous if you're caught outside. Hail ranges in size from tiny specks to the size of a baseball.

In 2024, hailstorms caused over a billion dollars in damage in the USA. Climate change is likely to increase the size of hail in the future. Increased warming may also reduce the number of hailstorms that have small hail, as small hail will melt faster in warmer temperatures.

SAFETY DURING HAILSTORMS Make sure you are in a sturdy building and away from windows. If you are caught outside, make sure you protect your head.

Blizzards and freezes

Even though the Earth is warming, blizzards and freezes can result from instability caused by climate change. Blizzards and freezes can make roads dangerous to drive on and cause accidents, damage important infrastructure like electrical grids and bridges, and cause roofs to collapse from the weight of snow. Cold weather can also be very dangerous to people if they are not prepared for the low temperatures.

In February 2021, several winter storms hit Texas, an area that does not usually freeze very often. Three different winter storms came together at the same time and caused lots of damage. The storms were so intense that a lot of people lost power, making heat, food, and water very difficult for a lot of people.

SAFETY DURING BLIZZARDS AND FREEZES

Make sure you have plenty of blankets and other ways to keep warm. Storing food, using towels to block drafts, and making sure pipes don't freeze are also important.

Creating Resilience for Severe Weather

The possibility of severe weather can be scary. Severe weather can hurt our communities and damage our homes.

The good news is that human beings have always been dealing with harsh weather, and when faced with a massive loss, we know how to rebuild and support our communities. One of humanity's greatest traits is resilience.

Resilience means the ability to come back from something hard. When you think of resilience, think of a rubber band. Rubber bands are very resilient because when you stretch them, they snap back to how they used to be. Glass, on the other hand, is not resilient. If you stress glass, it easily shatters, and you can't put it back together again.

Unfortunately, we will not be able to make the weather less intense or less variable. And even if we stop emitting excess greenhouse gases tomorrow, we will still have to deal with the extreme weather we have now. The best thing we can do in the face of increased extreme weather is to increase our resilience.

Resilience looks different depending on what kind of extreme weather a place usually gets. For places that are dealing with hotter and longer heatwaves, cities and other organizations set up heat stations, with cool water and shade. For a coastal community that is seeing more and more floods, increased resilience means adapting homes or creating buffer zones to allow wetlands and dunes to take the bulk of flood waters.

One of the best and easiest ways to create resilience in your community is to get to know your neighbors. When you know the people around you, and they know you, you can all protect each other more. When you know your upstairs neighbor is elderly and doesn't have air conditioning, you can help and check in on them during heatwaves, making sure they are cool enough. If you are caught unprepared by a flood, your neighbors will know to check in on you and get you help if you need it.

Other Climate Impacts

Severe weather is a common impact of climate change, but there are other impacts important to pay attention to. All the following things are directly impacted by climate change, and all can be dangerous.

WILDFIRES

Wildfires are scary and can be very dangerous. Like severe weather, wildfires are a natural part of the Earth. Wildfires of the past helped keep forests healthy and not overcrowded with dead trees. Some plants can only grow after a fire. These natural fires were usually kind of small and wouldn't get too hot, meaning that the taller and older trees wouldn't burn very much and would survive.

However, just like severe weather, wildfires have grown more frequent and more intense because of climate change. Wildfires have been growing in size in the US and have begun occurring well outside of the traditional "fire season." Droughts and heat waves have been becoming more frequent and harsher, making it easier for forests to burn.

The more that forests burn, the less habitat there is for nature. Also, fires have been getting closer to population centers where people live. In addition, when trees burn, greenhouse gases are emitted, and those trees can no longer store carbon.

Solutions

Firefighters are heroes who keep us safe when wildfires get out of control.

There are also ways to prepare for wildfires in advance. This is called fire management. Fire management can protect people and keep fires smaller so that they act like the fires of the past again.

Proper fire management is something that firefighters and professionals who work in our national parks and forests know how to do. A lot of the best ways we know to manage fires comes from knowledge taught by Indigenous people. Indigenous tribes managed forests for centuries, and some still do today.

Proper fire management includes "prescribed burns," where professionals light a fire to burn the deadwood in an area, while making sure it doesn't grow to be too strong. Once an area has burned a little, it is much less likely to burn again for a while, so this can keep fires from starting. Also, keeping landscapes as hydrated (wet) as possible means they are less likely to burn fast and hot.

There are also many things ordinary people can do to be prepared for wildfires. People in wildfire-prone areas are encouraged to keep "go bags" (a bag of essential items) in case they need to evacuate quickly. People in areas prone to fires can also "fire harden" their homes. This means they get rid of the things that can burn easily in their yards, and plant plants that don't burn easily. It's also important for home-owners to consider making upgrades to defend their roof, vents, and the rest of the house from fires.

This all keeps communities safer.

MELTING ICE

Ice exists on the planet in three main forms: glaciers, ice sheets, and sea ice. Warmer temperatures mean that the ice around the planet is melting. At the north and south poles, it is normal for ice to melt and refreeze along with the seasons. However, we are seeing ice re-freezing less, especially in the north, because of climate change.

Polar amplification describes the way that the polar regions are warming at a faster rate than the rest of the planet. It is estimated that the polar regions are warming twice as fast as the rest of the planet. This means that the ice in many parts of these regions is in danger of melting.

There are two main reasons Earth's ice melting is so harmful to the planet's health. First, when ice melts, it

turns into water and mixes into the ocean. If all the ice at the north and south poles of the planet melted, the ocean levels would rise a huge amount.

The second reason is a bit more surprising. It's called the **albedo**

effect. The albedo effect describes how the sun's light and heat reflect off light-colored surfaces. If you wear a black shirt on a hot sunny day, your shirt is going to absorb more heat. If you wear a white shirt on the same hot day, the white will reflect more of the sun's rays, and you will feel a little cooler. The same is true for the Earth. Since ice is white, it reflects the sun's rays. When it melts into the ocean, the same area that used to be white is now ocean blue, which is darker. When there is less ice, then less of the sun's heat is reflected out into space, and instead is absorbed into the ocean, trapping more heat.

Solutions

It's hard to stop ice from melting. But there are ways to increase the albedo effect in places other than the poles. Scientists have started recommending people paint the roofs of buildings white to increase the albedo effect and reflect more of the sun's heat back into space in non-polar spaces. Not only will this keep the Earth cooler, but it will keep the house cooler on a hot day, saving money and energy.

OCEAN RISE

Our oceans are one of Earth's most important resources. Algae in the ocean convert CO_2 into oxygen that we can breathe. One in three people across the world eats fish as their main source of protein, and fish live and thrive in the ocean. Ocean currents are incredibly important for shipping, as they make moving goods across the ocean faster and more efficient, and the world's largest trade centers are usually located near the ocean (or another water source). Because of these benefits, around one-third of the world's population lives near an ocean coast.

Oceans are incredibly important to our way of life. The ocean, as we know it, is also at risk from climate change. One of the ways the ocean is affected by climate change is through sea-level rise. We have been measuring sea-level rise since 1880. In 2023, the oceans were 8–9 inches higher than they were in 1880.

A few inches may not sound like very much, but since the ground near coasts is often flat beach, 1 inch of sea-level rise can cover up to 50–100 inches of ground. In the USA, around 30% of people live near the coast, meaning that a few inches of sea level rise will put many homes at risk of flooding.

Sea-level rise happens in two different ways. The first is through melting ice. The second is through heat. As ocean water gets warmer, it expands a little. Because there is so much water in the

ocean, this expansion can cause the oceans to rise even higher. The hotter the planet gets, the more the oceans will rise.

Solutions

People like living near the ocean, and they don't always want to leave to move away. To adapt to sea level rise, people sometimes raise their houses and their roads so that the more water comes, they will stay dry.

Another way to help manage sea level rise is through wetland ecosystems. Wetlands, like marshes and mangroves, hold a lot of water in their vegetation and their spongy soils. If we protect the wetland habitats

that already exist, we can help avoid the worst parts of sea level rise. Some communities are even planting or restoring more of these coastal ecosystems to help protect people's homes from storms.

OCEAN ACIDIFICATION

Remember that the ocean is part of the hydrosphere, and the hydrosphere is a station for greenhouse gases. The ocean stores a lot of carbon dioxide and keeps it out of the atmosphere. Without the ocean storing this carbon dioxide, we would see even more severe climate impacts.

However, the more carbon dioxide the ocean stores, the more acidic it becomes. In chemistry, almost all liquids can be sorted on a pH scale that goes from

acidic to basic (acids and bases are characteristics of chemicals). The scale runs from 0–14; water is usually right in the middle, at around a 7. Numbers below 7 are acidic, and numbers above 7 are basic.

Normally, seawater is slightly basic, but climate change has been making the water more acidic. When the ocean becomes more acidic, the creatures in the ocean that rely on shells or coral get stressed, as acid can start to eat away at their shells. And if the shells and coral are not doing well, this also harms people, as fishing harvests usually decrease when shellfish and coral struggle.

Solutions

Many people are concerned about ocean acidification, especially people who fish or otherwise get food or money from the ocean. There are many ocean acidification networks out there that educate people widely on ocean acidification. Some also restore and protect the ecosystems that are the most vulnerable to acidification, such as coral reefs, which helps keep the ocean healthier.

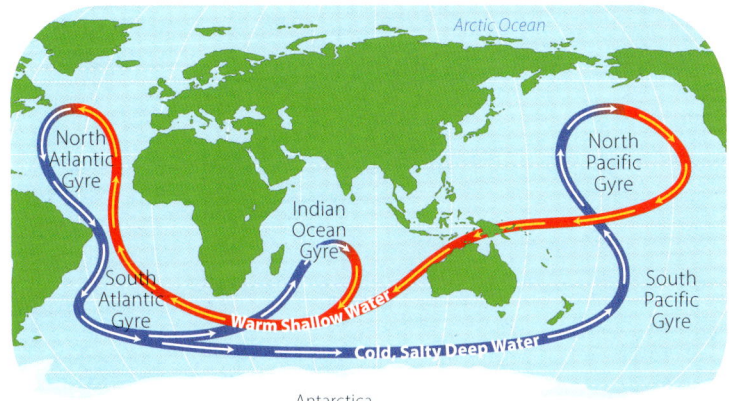

Antarctica

CURRENT LOSS

The ocean is full of currents or channels where water continuously flows. Ocean currents carry heat all over the planet and are one of the biggest regulators of Earth's temperature. Earth's currents are the main reason so many places are currently livable for humans. Without the ocean's currents, the Earth would be a very different place.

Climate change is slowing some ocean currents. As the ocean warms, certain currents have slowed down. Scientists are worried that with enough warming, some of the ocean's currents will stop, and this would be a disaster. It would likely change a lot about the Earth's climates: places used to having a lot of rain might not get it anymore, and places that are used to only a little rain may get flooded out.

The halting of currents, as far as scientists can tell, is still far away, but they have observed currents weakening and slowing down, which is not good.

Solutions

Stopping the amount of greenhouse gases entering the atmosphere is the main way to protect our oceans. Anything that can be done to decrease the amount of warming on the planet will help maintain the currents as well.

BIODIVERSITY LOSS

Biodiversity goes hand in hand with a stable and healthy climate. But what is biodiversity?

Biodiversity means the amount of different life forms existing in one area. A rainforest, with thousands of kinds of trees, plants, bugs, reptiles, birds, mammals, and fish, is considered very biodiverse. A farm that only ever grows one kind of corn in a field is not biodiverse. It doesn't matter how many ears of corn are in that field; they are all the same kind of plant, so the field is not biodiverse.

The Earth's climate drives biodiversity. The areas with the most biodiversity tend to be in the warmer, wet areas near the equator, or areas with Mediterranean climates like California. Areas that are cold, with less accessible water, like the Arctic tundra, have less biodiversity because the plants and animals that live in that environment have to be highly specialized to survive there.

Biodiversity can be lost. Ecosystems and habitats where creatures live can change as the climate changes, and something that used to be comfortable there may no longer be able to live there.

Take wood frogs, for example. Over winter, wood frogs can freeze solid to wait until the spring, since there are not many bugs for them to eat over winter. But if it no longer gets cold enough for wood frogs to freeze over the winter, they are left awake and looking for food when no insects are available. Their population may not bounce back.

Overhunting and the introduction of invasive species also cause biodiversity loss, and it's important to remember that biodiversity loss isn't occurring only because of climate change. However, climate change does make it harder for populations of plants and wildlife to recover from major losses.

Solutions

Protecting habitats, like forests, prairies, and marshes, from being turned into farms or neighborhoods can help protect biodiversity. Not only does this protect biodiversity, but it also protects the plants that are able to sequester carbon.

Another solution to help biodiversity is helping to reintroduce environmental engineers and keystone species to areas. These are species that may have been driven out of their habitat, or overhunted, and need to be reintroduced to an area.

Environmental engineers are species that, when introduced to a habitat, shape their environment around them, and make space livable for other species as well. Beavers are a great example of an environmental engineer. Beavers are famous for building dams, and those dams enable tons of species of plants, fish, insects, amphibians, mammals, and more to thrive around them!

Keystone species are species that many other parts of an ecosystem rely on. Wolves are a great example of a keystone species. When an area has too many deer that are eating too many plants in an area, deer become a threat to the biodiversity of the plants. When wolves are reintroduced and hunt some of the deer, the plants can recover, and the whole ecosystem is balanced and able to work together.

FOOD LOSS

Whether you like pizza, grilled cheese, soup, steak, or salads, all the ingredients for our food come from the Earth. Even if you eat a lot of meat, nearly all meat products depend directly on plants. Think of the grain that cows or pigs eat. Unfortunately, climate change affects the way crops grow, impacting our ability to grow food.

The increased variability of weather makes it harder for us to predict rainfall. For example, the climate in a certain area may have received rain once a week, on average, which was great for growing crops. However, with climate change, weather is less dependable and more highly variable, meaning water is harder to come by and crops may wither.

If plant crops are withering, not only do we have less food to eat, but we also have less to feed livestock, meaning we'll also have less meat. Drier and hotter conditions can also lead to more diseases or pests that hurt crops, and these diseases can wipe out whole fields of the same crop.

Solutions

Climate-friendly practices for farming help protect the crops, as well as keep greenhouse gas emissions down. By growing a lot of different foods, one disease cannot wipe out an entire field, and this also keeps the soil healthier.

Reducing food waste is another way to use the most out of what we already grow. Properly storing food and being strategic about how you shop for food means less food and less waste, which is helpful if there are food supply problems.

FRESHWATER LOSS

Every creature on Earth needs water to live, and every person needs freshwater to drink, and stay clean and healthy

Glaciers, snow, and other icy parts of the world are important for freshwater flow. Many water systems rely on water that comes from snowmelt and glacier melt. As the snow and glaciers melt, the water travels down to less cool areas where humans and animals live. However, as the planet warms, there is less snow, and it melts more quickly, and the people who depend on that water have less water available. We're already seeing this in places like California.

Climate change also increases the need for water, as people need to drink water to deal with the heat, but this can also mean that we use up our stores of water faster than they can be naturally replenished. Droughts make this a higher risk, as water can't be replenished as we use the water to grow crops and in our daily lives.

Water quality is also expected to get worse because of climate change. Stronger storms that dump a lot of rain at once can lead to more sediments in runoff before they reach water storage. Rising sea levels are also causing saltwater intrusion. Saltwater intrusion is when saltwater from the ocean contaminates freshwater sources, making them unhealthy to drink.

Solutions

Reducing water waste and conserving what freshwater we have will keep more freshwater available, and those are healthy habits to know when there is a freshwater shortage.

Helping to protect freshwater ecosystems, like marshes and streams, also helps conserve our water supply. Freshwater ecosystems help replenish the amount of freshwater in our groundwater and water storage, so keeping these ecosystems healthy means more freshwater for us as well.

HEALTH IMPACTS

Climate change carries a lot of risks that can be hazardous to our health. Severe weather is an obvious danger, and so are food or water shortages. But climate change can also lead to new or more widespread diseases.

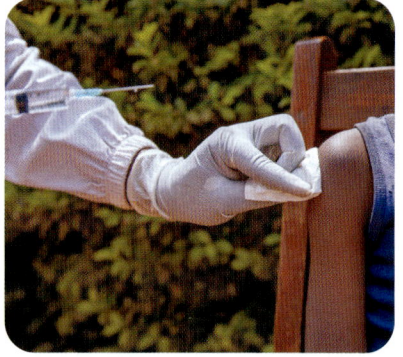

For example, there are illnesses, such as malaria, that used to be confined to certain parts of the tropics and subtropics, but as the world grows warmer, malaria has been spreading. Similarly, tick-borne diseases have been spreading, as wood ticks have been expanding their range due to warming temperatures.

Solutions

Reducing greenhouse gases in the atmosphere and limiting climate change is the best solution we have to protect against the negative health impacts. There are also other choices that can protect people's health while fighting climate change. For example, transitioning from gasoline-powered cars to electric cars reduces the air pollution that hurts people's lungs.

Technology that can help preserve food, water, and medicine in the face of variable temperatures and harsh weather will help keep people fed and healthy as well.

CLIMATE JUSTICE

Climate change wasn't caused by everyone equally. In fact, most people alive today are not responsible for why climate change is so severe right now. In fact, some of the people and countries that are least responsible for climate change are seeing some of the worst impacts. That isn't fair.

For example, consider the Maldives. It is the smallest country in Asia. It has an incredibly small carbon footprint compared to the other countries in the world, but the Maldives is in trouble. If greenhouse gases continue filling the atmosphere, and warming grows stronger, the Maldives will be underwater soon because of rising sea levels. To highlight this problem, the Maldives held a conference underwater (wearing full scuba gear), calling for action on climate change around the world, to show that their home is at risk because of the choices of other nations. Even though the Maldives has done very little to cause climate change, it is dealing with some of the worst consequences.

Many countries that are responsible for a lot of emissions don't want to change because they could lose money. However, when you think about saving the many people in the world threatened by climate change, money doesn't actually seem very important.

Solutions

Centering climate solutions on people who need them most, first, is a great way to help create more justice. For example, if a neighborhood was built next to a busy road and now has bad air quality issues, there are solutions. The city should provide electric buses for that neighborhood to help reduce air pollution before giving those buses to other neighborhoods.

The United States is one of the countries that has emitted the most carbon emissions in the world, which means it is fair to demand change in America in order to protect everyone else. The more Americans who act to reduce greenhouse gases and reduce warming, the better for the planet and everyone on it.

What Can I Do?

Learning about the causes and impacts of climate change can feel overwhelming!

The good news is, it is not too late to act and avoid the worst impacts scientists have predicted from climate change. Many things must change for us to create a safe and livable future, and this future is within our reach.

DEBUNKING COMMON MYTHS ABOUT CLIMATE

Understanding climate change isn't easy. There are also a lot of people who are afraid of climate change or are afraid of the changes we need to make to fix it. Those people can sometimes lie or purposely mislead others about climate change.

Here are some common arguments people use to mislead others about climate change. If you see any of these arguments in real life, now you'll know what to say in response!

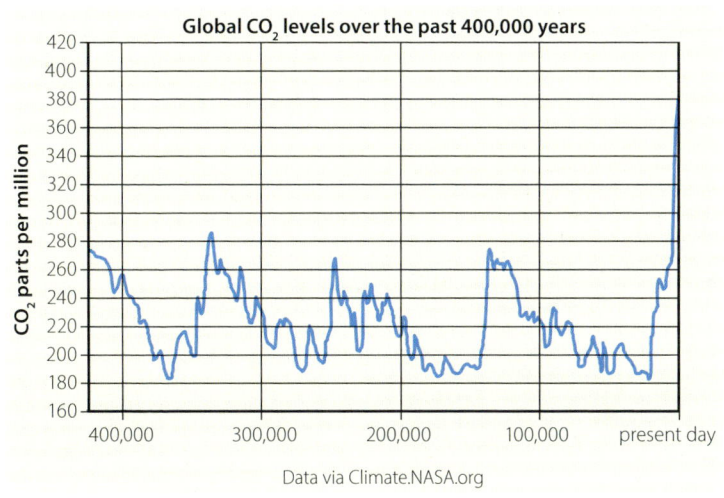

Data via Climate.NASA.org

"Isn't the Climate Always Changing?"

Some people argue that humans cannot be the cause of climate change because the climate of the planet has always been changing since it formed. While it is true that the Earth's climate has always been variable, we know that current climate change is human-caused.

This graph shows the levels of CO_2 in the atmosphere for the past 400,000 years. You can see that the levels of carbon dioxide have changed a lot over the past thousands of years.

But if you look closely, you will see that these changes follow a cycle until 1950. The 1950s are well into the time humans had been putting greenhouse gases into the atmosphere to make energy. You can see that from that point onward the carbon dioxide level skyrocketed to levels never seen in the previous 400,000 years.

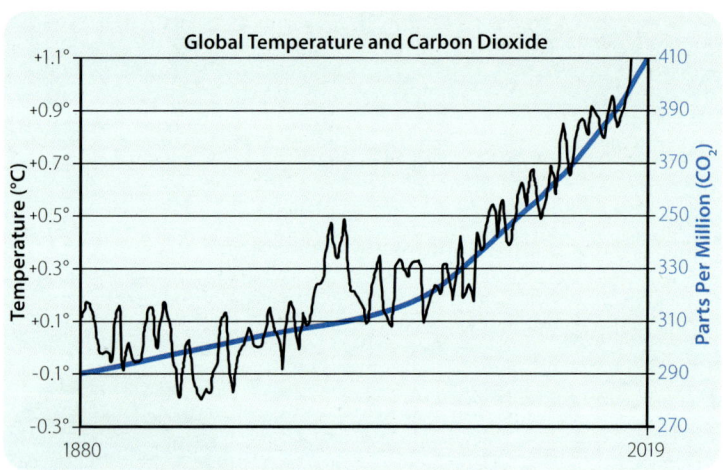

Looking at this graph, you will see that the increase in CO_2 is causing a lot of warming. The amount of carbon dioxide in the atmosphere has risen steadily since 1880. The temperature line goes up and down a bit, but if you look closely, you'll see that it increases with carbon dioxide.

From these two graphs, we can see two things. First, we have more CO_2 in the atmosphere than the Earth has had in its atmosphere for hundreds of thousands of years. Second, we can see a consistent rise in temperatures with a rise in CO_2.

We can see that the Earth's climate does change a little bit over long periods of time. We can also see that the Earth has never changed in the same way that it is changing now. This drastic and recent change matches with when human beings have been mining and burning fossil fuels from the ground.

"Isn't it the Sun?"

Some doubters think the sun is to blame for the recent heating. While the sun's heat is ultimately what is trapped by greenhouse gases and creates warming, the sun's activity is not responsible for our current warming.

Doubters suggest that an increase in activity from the sun is causing warming in a temporary cycle. That's not true. We've been monitoring the sun closely from space for almost 50 years, and we haven't seen any unusual activity. These arguments try to take the responsibility away from carbon-producing sources and effectively blame the sun to make humans innocent when it comes to climate change.

Scientists, time and time again, have proved that the sun's own cycles don't really affect the temperature on Earth all that much.

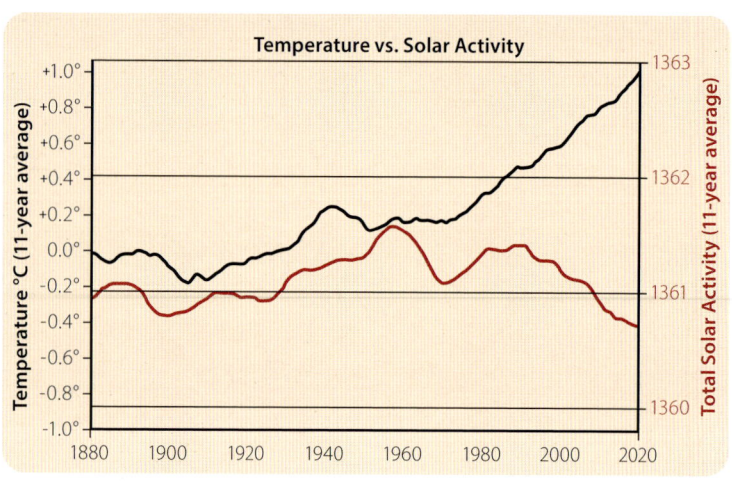

This graph shows solar activity compared to global temperature on Earth. If this argument were true, and the sun is what is heating the Earth more recently, then we would see the lines stay together the whole graph. However, in the graph, we see the lines move away from each other at the end. Since this means the sun's activity and global temperature aren't directly connected, there must be something else increasing global temperature. The answer: greenhouse gases.

"What About the Scientists Who Don't Agree?"

You may hear the occasional scientist say that climate change isn't caused by fossil fuels, or that it won't be harmful. But those scientists are in a tiny minority.

Overall, 97% of scientists believe that climate change is happening now and that it is caused by human actions. This is a very high number. This means for every 100 scientists, only 3 don't believe in climate change. If all 97 scientists agree, and only 3 disagree, then the voices that agree must have a point.

An important part of science is that it is peer-reviewed. This means when a scientist wants to publish their findings on climate change, other scientists repeat their experiments or look at the papers that the scientists read, to make sure that the research is correct. While scientists are often very good at their jobs, they can still have their own biases, and peer review helps make sure that those biases don't get in the way of good science.

However, sometimes people just want to harm the science that 97% of scientists believe. Here are important questions to ask when someone is trying to make people doubt scientists and their experiments:

- Are they being paid? Do they work for a company that might lose money from climate-positive actions, like a fossil fuel company?

- Are they arguing honestly about the subject (climate science), or is their main goal simply to turn people against the science? One way to tell is if they are outright lying or simply ignore evidence in favor of insults, bullying, or talking points.

- Does the person have a science background of any kind? Is it in a relevant field? If not, why consider their opinion? (Someone informed in the field seems a better option.)

- Do they have a strong bias in their work or views?

TAKING CARE OF YOURSELF AND OTHERS

How to Handle Hard Topics

Climate change isn't an easy thing to think about. When it gets too hard to think about and you feel overwhelmed, try a few different things to re-center yourself.

Identify your feelings
Are you feeling sad? Angry? Stressed? Worried? Take time to breathe and try to name the emotion you are feeling.

Talk to a trusted adult
The adults in our lives are there for us to go to with our problems. If you ever get overwhelmed with thoughts about climate change, go to an adult

you trust. They can help you manage what you are feeling. Find a teacher, parent, guardian, therapist, or other trustworthy person whom you feel comfortable talking about your feelings with, and let them know that you need help.

Do something else

Climate change is a big problem, and it's going to take time to solve it. If you ever get overwhelmed, then take a break. Do something else you enjoy, like reading, hiking, playing a game, or seeing your friends. Let yourself think about something else and calm down. There are thousands of other people in the world helping to solve climate change, so when you need a break, give yourself a break, and let them take over for a while. Then, when you're ready to act, do it!

Looking Out for Your Neighbors

One of the strongest tools we have as humans is community. Looking out for the people in your community, your family, friends, and neighbors is very important. Climate change affects all of us, and when we prepare for some negative impacts, it's always a good thing to check on the others around you. Are they prepared? Are they safe?

Educating those around you about what you know about climate change is a good way to prepare others. This can also build trust in your community, which is important when you work together. This can help strengthen your ability to cut your community's carbon footprint or prepare for a harsh storm on the way.

Small Steps Every Day

Many people say that taking small steps every day to ensure a greener planet helps them feel more in control and happier. Things like riding their bike to school instead of in a car, or getting signatures on a petition to get compost bins for their neighborhood. Taking small actions every day can help people feel in control in a world that is changing.

Sometimes, the best thing you can do in a day is go on to the next one. If you are having a day where everything is hard, including school, home, friends, or anything else, the best thing you can do is try again tomorrow.

If you are ever stressed about the state of the planet, but you, for any reason, feel like you have not "done anything," remember this: There are so many people out there doing good.

There are people in your town planting trees. There are people in your state creating more green jobs. There are people in your country who are cutting down on their fossil fuel use. There are people all over the world who are doing the right thing and making progress for the planet, and it's okay if you don't. Because one day, if you do something, they will be able to take a break and rest easy knowing that you are helping the planet.

We are in this together, and more is happening than you will ever know.

Activities

COMMUNITY SCIENCE

Scientists need data to find out how the world works. When it comes to climate, the more data, the better! Do some community science to help keep the scientists up to date!

Community science is when ordinary people gather data in their everyday lives and record it so that it's able to be used in experiments later. It is usually based around observations.

There are many great apps for citizen science, and here are just a few that can help scientists looking to help the planet!

iNaturalist for uploading photos of plants, animals, and fungi you observe, which can help track the effects of climate change

Project Noah, run by National Geographic, for documenting lots of different kinds of organisms

NASA Globe Clouds for taking pictures of clouds and uploading them to help scientists use with their satellite data about our weather and climate

Project Budburst documenting when plants bloom and go through other seasonal transformations to see if climate change is affecting their cycles

mPING for submitting what weather is happening right now where you are. Used by NOAA and the NWS to analyze the accuracy of their weather forecasts

MEASURING CLIMATE THROUGH CRAFTS

The reason we know so much about where the climate has been and where it is going is because scientists have been recording temperatures for centuries. And we can always use more data! But collecting data doesn't have to just be written down on a piece of paper; it can be colorful!

You can use all kinds of different crafts for this project. Some people have made temperature blankets, some people make temperature scarves, or murals. In this activity, we'll demonstrate how to track climate data on a piece of paper, but if you have another craft form you love or want to try, go ahead and adapt this to it!

Supplies: graph paper, notebook, and colored pencils.

The first thing you want to do is define your colors. Traditionally, people use colors going from red (hot) to blue (cold), but you can use whatever you want. The next step is to make a key.

A key is something you're going to reference throughout the year (or the time period you're doing this project in) to keep the project going, so it's very important to keep it where you can find it.

In your key, you will assign a color to every 5 degrees F (or 1 degree C). Write down next to a swatch of color what temperature range that color represents. Remember, over the course of the year, you're going to represent that temperature with that color!

Next, start writing down in a separate page of the notebook the highest temperature for every day. If you have a thermometer outside your

Date	Temp	Range
4/3/25	47	46-50
4/4/25	52	51-55
4/5/25	44	41-45
4/6/25	60	56-60
4/7/25	40	36-40
4/8/25	49	46-50
4/9/25	62	61-65
4/10/25	50	46-50
4/11/25	57	56-60
4/12/25	70	66-70
4/13/25	68	66-70
4/14/25	55	51-55
4/15/25	55	51-55
4/16/25	60	56-60
4/17/25	75	71-75
4/18/25	60	56-60
4/19/25	55	51-55
4/20/25	55	51-55
4/21/25	62	61-65
4/22/25	70	66-70
4/23/25	69	66-70
4/24/25	52	51-55
4/25/25	59	56-60
4/26/25	62	61-65
4/27/25	65	61-65
4/28/25	73	71-75
4/29/25	59	56-60
4/30/25	69	66-70
5/1/25	65	61-65
5/2/25	50	46-50
5/3/25	66	66-70
5/4/25	81	81-85
5/5/25	76	76-80
5/6/25	83	81-85
5/7/25	72	71-75
5/8/25	72	71-75
5/9/25	85	81-85
5/10/25	75	71-75
5/11/25	90	86-90
5/12/25	87	86-90

house in a window, make sure you document the highest it gets over the course of that day. Otherwise, you can look online at your local weather station to see what the highest temperature was.

On your project paper, color in one line with the corresponding color for the temperature it was that day. For example, if the high for the day was 77 degrees F, then you would use the color you set aside for 75–80 degrees F. Make sure you write down the high temperature every day that you can, and you can always color in multiple days at the same time later.

Over time, what does it look like? When you look at other people's temperature projects from earlier years, do the colors look different? Why or why not?

Can you tell where the seasons are based on the colors?

At the end of the year, you will have officially measured your own microclimate! Measuring and documenting the temperature record for specific areas, like where you live, is important for scientists, as many scientists can't go out and measure every spot on Earth. So, if a scientist ever comes around trying to document your area's microclimate, you will have a colorful and helpful documentation of the whole year you did the project!

IMAGINE A BETTER FUTURE: WHAT COULD GO HERE?

Supplies: pencil, paper; optional: printer

The more you learn about climate impacts in your local area, the more you might want to make a change! Maybe you have a wide road near you that doesn't have any protected bike lanes. Maybe you know that there is not enough tree cover around your neighborhood to prevent it from warming up a lot in the summer (known as the urban heat island effect).

One option is to turn a weedy lawn into a spot for native plants

Activity: Go around your neighborhood and see where areas could be improved. Use your imagination! Maybe a rain garden can go in a grassy lot, or fruit trees could be planted along a sidewalk. You could even take a picture of an area that could use sustainable improvements and draw your climate solutions over the photo!

Obviously, you need permission to make changes to land owned by others, but every climate solution we have exists because someone imagined it. Honing the power of your imagination to change the world for the better is one of the best things you can do.

JOINING A COMMUNITY GARDEN

A lot of people who care about climate projects like to go to community gardens. Community gardens are spaces where people who don't necessarily have access to green space of their own can come together and grow things with each other.

A thriving urban garden

Community gardens are great spaces to meet people who also care about the planet, plant gorgeous plants to watch grow, and even eat their tasty fruits and have a peaceful space to hang out in a neighborhood.

Community gardens also often have events. Some gardens can have days where they teach the community about the power of planting native plants. They might even give away seeds for you to plant somewhere else!

Get with a trusted adult, and search online for community gardens in your area. You can also go to your local library and ask the librarian, or look at their community board, as community gardens often use libraries as partners.

If you can't find a community garden in your area, is there a plot of land near you that isn't serving a purpose? Sometimes, you can find a group already working to turn that empty lot into a community garden. They might need more hands and voices of support, and that's where you can help! Maybe you can lend a hand in building a community garden in your neighborhood!

CALCULATE YOUR ENERGY USE

Are you curious about the carbon footprint of your home or school? One way to start finding it out is by calculating your energy use.

Tools and Materials:
- Calculator
- Computer
- Pencil and Paper

Find a building that you want to calculate energy use in. Then start identifying things that use energy. Count the lightbulbs and write down how many there are. Count the refrigerators, heaters, and anything else you find.

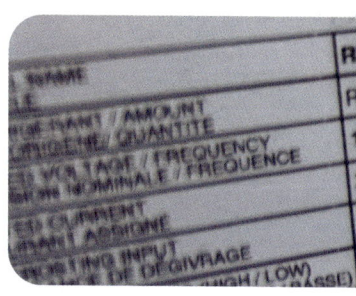

To figure out an appliance's power usage, look for a label or model number, and then head online.

Then, after writing all that down, go to the internet and search how much energy those things usually use. (You might need to look for model numbers/labels on each item and search that way.) Add up all the energy used in a calculator. Now you know roughly how much energy is used!

Remember, measuring your energy use is important, but remember that trying to make your house net-zero won't be the only thing to save the world. Your house is likely always going to use energy. The buildings that hold more than just your family, like schools and businesses, use more resources than your house. If you've found places to cut energy use and save money in your house, then that's great! But it makes a much bigger impact if you can join other people to petition your school or another community building to go green.

CLIMATE SURVEY

A lot of climate-positive infrastructure already exists in the world. Let's see if there's anything in your neighborhood!

Supplies: notebook, pen/pencil; optional: map

Go on a walk (with a trusted adult) and see if you can spot any climate projects in the world! If you're walking around a neighborhood, you may see people who have put solar panels on their houses or have planted gardens for habitat. Write down what you see.

Solar Panels on a residential house

If you're in a denser area, there's still some climate infrastructure you can see! Bus stops and train stations are climate infrastructure, as they help reduce greenhouse gas emissions from cars. There might be signs that say "congestion zone," or trees planted along the sidewalk. Maybe you'll see electric car charging stations. As you keep taking walks, note the new things you spot, and you'll get to watch the world install climate-positive projects in real time!

If you really want a detailed look at your neighborhood's climate infrastructure, you can print out a map of your neighborhood and use your notes to draw where you saw gardens, solar panels, or bus stops. Looking at the map, are there any places where you think your neighborhood could use more climate-smart projects? Consider writing to someone in local government, tell them that you have surveyed your neighborhood, and you would like to propose that they install a pollinator garden, plant some trees, or build solar panels. Who knows? You might make change in your own neighborhood!

CREATE POSITIVE LAND USE CHANGE!

Land use change is the second-largest source of carbon emissions, but there is positive land use change, too! Changing a lawn or barren patch of ground into a habitat is a way to positively impact the world around you.

Milkweed in a container garden

If you have a yard, look at how much lawn you have. Ask your parents if there is an area in your yard that could have a tree, some bushes, or wildflowers instead. Changing parts of your lawn into space for different plants can save water, create habitat for local wildlife, and save your parents from mowing that spot!

If you don't have a yard, see if there's any outdoor space you can use to plant something on. Using pots on a fire escape or your front steps is a way to provide habitat for pollinators, and, if you use compost from the store or from a local community garden, then you can sequester a little more carbon dioxide from the air the more the plant grows.

Something fun you can do, if you do create some positive land use change, is register your yard on homegrownnationalpark.com!

If you don't have a fire escape, front porch, or any outdoor space where you could plant something, then look around your community! Libraries and community gardens often let volunteers come and plant things in a shared space. Often, these places also share compost or native seeds for free!

There are also neighborhood beautification groups that you could volunteer with to help create positive land use change. If there are unused parts of a neighborhood where scrub grass just grows and isn't used for much, then neighborhoods sometimes get together to plant a shared, beautiful landscape where nothing was happening before. See if your neighborhood or town has any groups that do work like this and see if you can volunteer! If you ever need volunteer hours for school, these are great projects to be involved in, and they're fun!

Growing and giving away native plants is a great project for groups

START A GROUP

There are a lot of great groups working to clean up their homes, parks, and communities. But not every area has a group with exactly what you are looking for. When this happens, it might be a good idea to start your own group.

Local libraries are a great resource to start with when you want to start a group. Librarians can help you find a place to meet, whether inside the library or out, and offer other resources as you begin.

When designing a group to meet, it's important to ask yourself these questions:

What do you want your group to do?

When and how often would you meet?

How many people do you want in your group?

When you have these questions answered, go out and start looking for other group members! It doesn't matter if your group starts small. Once you start doing activities, other people might see you and become interested in what you are doing. Then, you'll get to invite them in!

Sources

To save paper—and trees!—the source material for this book is available online at this permanent link: advkeen.co/climate_sources.

Glossary

A

Acid rain: Rain that contains harmful chemicals, made when certain air pollutants mix with water in the sky, usually caused by burning coal.

Adaptation: When a plant, animal, or person changes how they live to handle new conditions. Many creatures will have to adapt to climate impacts.

Aerosols: Tiny solid particles that float in the air.

Agriculture: The science of raising crops and animals for food and other resources

Albedo Effect: Describes how the sun's light bounces off light-colored surfaces, like white ice, and goes back into space, contributing less warming to the planet.

Atmosphere: The layer of gases around Earth that lets us breathe, blocks harmful UV rays, and maintains a comfortable temperature for life to thrive.

B

Battery storage: Big batteries that save extra electricity (for example, from solar or wind) to use later.

Biodiversity: The variety of living things in one place, including plants, animals, fungi, and microscopic creatures.

Biogas: Gas made when waste or dead plants decompose. Biogas can be used to generate energy.

Biomass: Plant material (like wood or crop leftovers) burned for energy or heat.

Biosphere: All the living things on Earth, including plants, animals, fungi, and people. One of the "stations" for carbon.

Blizzard: A severe storm with strong winds, cold temperatures, and lots of snow.

C

Carbon: A common element found on planet Earth.

Carbon cycle: The way carbon moves through all the "spheres."

Carbon dioxide (CO_2): The most common greenhouse gas, made of carbon and oxygen.

Carbon footprint: The amount of greenhouse gases a person, community, or activity puts into the atmosphere.

Carbon sequestration: When excess carbon leaves the atmosphere and goes into a different "sphere."

Carbon sink: Places that store carbon when it is taken out of the atmosphere, like trees or soil.

Carbon source: Something that releases carbon into the atmosphere, like burning fuel or rotting wood.

Chlorofluorocarbons (CFCs): Chemicals that made a hole in the ozone layer; their use was limited in products after we learned the damage they caused.

Citizen science: When regular people help scientists by observing and recording data.

Circular economy: A system where we reduce, reuse, repair, and recycle so we waste less and cause less pollution.

Climate: A consistent set of conditions on Earth, including temperature, rain, pressure, and wind, that are present over a long period of time.

Climate change: Changes in the Earth's climate that lead to more variable and intense weather, caused by human actions.

Climate justice: Considering communities that are harmed by climate change the worst and making sure that climate solutions are fair to those communities.

Coal: A solid fossil fuel that is found underground and is considered the dirtiest of the fossil fuels.

Compost: Plant waste and food scraps that have decomposed into soil fertilizer.

Coral: Small ocean animals that build reefs, which are hurt by warm and acidic ocean water.

Cryosphere: All the frozen water on Earth, like ice caps and glaciers.

D

Decomposition: When plants or animals break down after they die, returning nutrients and gases from the biosphere to other "spheres."

Deforestation: Cutting down or burning forests.

Drought: A long period of time with much less rain than is normal for that area.

E

Ecologist: A scientist who studies how living things interact with each other and their environment.

Ecosystem: The web of relationships between living things that live in a specific location.

Electric vehicle (EV): A vehicle powered by electricity instead of a fossil fuel.

Emissions: Gases released into the atmosphere (like carbon dioxide).

Energy mix: The different energy sources a place uses (like wind, solar, and gas).

Environmental engineer: A species, like beavers, that changes its habitat in ways that help many others.

Evacuation order: A message from officials telling people to leave an area to stay safe from a disaster.

F

Fertilizer: Nutrients added to soil to help plants grow.

Flash flood: A flood that happens very quickly, making it hard to prepare for.

Flood: Water covering land that's usually dry.

Fossil fuels: Energy sources like coal, oil, and natural gas formed from ancient life. Burning them adds greenhouse gases to the atmosphere.

Freeze: A weather event that happens when the temperature drops very low. When severe enough, they can be a natural disaster.

G

Geologist: A scientist who studies the lithosphere and rocks.

Geothermal energy: Energy that comes from heat inside the Earth.

Glacier: A large mass of ice that can be found on land.

Global warming: The rise in Earth's average temperature caused by greenhouse gases.

Go-bag: A packed bag with supplies you need if you must leave quickly in an emergency.

Goldilocks Planet: A nickname for the Earth because its climate is "just right" for life.

Greenhouse effect: When greenhouse gases trap more of the Sun's heat, the more gases there are, the hotter the Earth gets.

Greenhouse gases (GHGs): Gases like CO_2, methane, and water vapor that trap heat in the atmosphere.

Great Green Wall: A project where 20 countries in Africa are planting trees to restore ecosystems.

H

Habitat: The natural home of a plant or animal.

Hail: Balls of ice that fall from clouds.

Heatwave: Severe weather where the average temperature is much higher than normal for a long time.

Hurricane: A powerful storm with strong winds and heavy rain that forms over warm ocean water.

Hydrologist: A scientist who studies water.

Hydropower: Energy made from moving water.

Hydrosphere: All the water on Earth: oceans, rivers, lakes, clouds, and groundwater.

I

Ice core: A long tube of ice drilled from glaciers or ice sheets that holds tiny bubbles of ancient air that scientists use to study the Earth.

Industry: Making materials and products in factories.

Invasive species: Plants or animals are introduced to a new area and harm local species.

J

Justice: Treating people fairly and meeting their needs, especially those most at risk.

K

Keystone species: A species that an ecosystem relies on to function properly.

L

Landfill: A large hole where trash is buried.

Land-use change: Changing nature into farms, roads, or buildings, which can harm habitats and release carbon.

Law of the Conservation of Matter: A rule of physics that matter cannot be created or destroyed, just changed into something else.

Linear economy: When people make something, use it once, and throw it away, instead of reusing the materials, contributing to pollution and waste.

Lithosphere: The part of the Earth containing solid rock, minerals, and other things in the ground, where most of the Earth's carbon lives.

M

Mangrove forest: A coastal biome that grows along shorelines and can protect land from harsh storms.

Methane (CH4): A strong greenhouse gas released by natural gas leaks, landfills, and even cow burps

Microclimate: The climate in a small area (like your neighborhood) that can differ from the larger region (like your state).

Monoculture: A farming practice where the farmer only grows one kind of crop.

Montreal Protocol: An international agreement that reduced the CFCs that damaged the ozone layer.

N

Natural gas: A fossil fuel used for electricity, heating, and cooking.

Net-zero: When a system stores just as many emissions as it releases.

Nitrous oxide (N_2O): A powerful greenhouse gas, often released by fertilizers.

Non-renewable energy: Energy forms like fossil fuels that are limited and can't be restored.

Nuclear energy: Non-renewable energy made by splitting atoms, usually from uranium.

O

Ocean acidification: The process of the ocean becoming more acidic due to climate change.

Ocean currents: Large flows of ocean water that move heat around the planet.

Oil: A fossil fuel used for fuel and products like plastics.

Ozone (O_3): A gas that is helpful or harmful depending on where it is. High in the atmosphere, it protects us from harmful UV rays, and at ground level, it's a pollutant.

Ozone layer: Part of the upper atmosphere that blocks most of the Sun's dangerous UV radiation.

P

Per capita: A way to measure "per person" by dividing by the number of people.

Pesticide: A chemical used to kill pests.

Photosynthesis: How plants use sunlight, water, and CO_2 to make food and release oxygen.

Polar amplification: The faster warming happening near Earth's poles compared to the rest of the planet.

Pollution: Harmful substances in the air, water, or soil.

Power plant: A place where electricity is made.

Prescribed burn: A planned, carefully controlled fire that reduces dry fuel to help prevent big wildfires.

R

Recycle: Turning used materials into new products.

Reduce: Buying or using less to make less waste and fewer emissions.

Renewable energy: Energy that doesn't run out, like solar or wind energy.

Reuse: Using something again instead of throwing it away after using it.

Reservoir: Another word for a "tank" or a holding place.

Resilience: The ability to bounce back after hard events, like severe storms.

S

Saltwater intrusion: When ocean water moves into freshwater sources and makes them unhealthy to drink.

Sea-level rise: Ocean levels getting higher due to melting ice and ocean water expanding.

Sector: A category of activities, like energy, transport, or agriculture, used to track emissions.

Sequestration: Removing and storing carbon from the atmosphere.

Severe weather: Dangerous weather like hurricanes, tornadoes, floods, heatwaves, and blizzards.

Solar energy: Electricity made by energy from the sun.

Spectroscopy: Shining light through air samples to see what gases and particles are inside.

Spheres: The big Earth systems: atmosphere, hydrosphere, cryosphere, lithosphere, and biosphere.

T

Topsoil: The rich, upper layer of soil that holds nutrients and stores carbon.

Tornado: A severe storm where a spinning column of air travels through an area.

Transport: How people and goods move around (cars, buses, trains, ships, planes).

Turbine: A machine that spins to make electricity.

U

Urban heat island: When cities are hotter than nearby areas because of dark surfaces and fewer trees.

V

Variable weather: Weather that is less predictable.

W

Waste: Things we throw away.

Water vapor: Water in gas form.

Weather: What is going on in the atmosphere during a short period of time.

Wetlands: Biomes that hold water, protect coasts, and support wildlife.

Wildfire: A fire that burns out of control in forests or grasslands.

Wind energy: Electricity made when wind turns turbine blades.

About the Author

Ian Hunt grew up in Ohio, where he enjoyed winters filled with snow and sledding. He became interested in climate change when he noticed those snowy winters becoming less frequent. He moved from the Midwest to California, where he held a variety of jobs, from hardening homes for fires, to planting native habitats. He earned his MA in Climate and Society from the Columbia University Climate School, and now resides in Brooklyn, where he is an advocate for climate education and climate action.

Credits continued from page 2

Ken Schulze: 123 (top); **khaligis:** 89 (bottom); **kristof lauwers:** 14 (bottom); **LanaElcova:** 31; **Lane V. Erickson:** 56; **leolintang:** 101; **Ljupco Smokovski:** 24 (right); **Louise_Michel:** 32 (top); **Luckyting:** 79; **m.malinika:** 95 (all); **MainlanderNZ:** 116 (top); **Maksim Safaniuk:** 55 (top, fossil fuels); **Manop Boonpeng:** 49 (bottom); **Manuel Weiter:** 47 (bottom); **Marc Rossmann:** 100; **Marco Ortiz-MOF:** 32 (middle); **MariuszKielbowicz:** 140 (bottom); **Matthew J Thomas:** 121 (top); **Me dia:** 36 (bottom); **Media Lens King:** 128 (bottom); **MILA PARH:** 11 (top); **mkfilm:** 99; **Mongkolchon Akesin:** 15 (top), 113 (top); **moomsabuy:** 90 (top); **Mozgova:** 46; **Najmi Arif:** 3 (water droplet); **Nancy Ann Bowe:** 142; **Neil Bowman:** 27 (bottom); **New Africa:** 88; **Nippani:** 74 (top); **Nmaneer:** 107; **Norman Allchin:** 38; **Ody_Stocker:** 24 (left); **ORION PRODUCTION:** 37 (bottom); **Oticki:** 83 (top); **PeopleImages:** 50 (bottom), 129, 131, 137, 152; **Peter Hermes Furian:** 18; **Peter Milto:** 82; **Pix One:** 61; **Piyaset:** 66 (bottom); **Poggensee:** 70; **Porstocker:** 1 & 3 (earth); **POV_artist:** 91 (bottom); **Rabbitmindphoto:** 45; **Rangsarit Chaiyakun:** 33; **Riderfoot:** 120; **Robert Wilder Jr:** 112 (top); **RossHelen:** 75; **Rsooll:** 125 (top); **Russamee:** 109; **Sally Hunter:** 47 (top); **saweang.w:** 89 (top); **Scharfsinn:** 71; **Scorpp:** 10; **Seplin1989:** 81; **SeventyFour:** 50 (top), 140 (middle); **SpeedKingz:** 140 (top); **Standret:** 50 (middle); **studio23:** 14 (top); **Svet foto:** 42; **T.W. van Urk:** 55 (top, renewable & bottom, wind); **TajdidProtik:** 122 (bottom); **Tapui:** 132; **Tato_Torrejon:** 92 (top); **TetiBond:** 43; **Tony LePrieur Photography:** 123 (bottom); **Travelwild:** 78; **ultramansk:** 67 (top); **Umomos:** 84 (middle); **VanderWolf Images:** 91 (top); **VectorMine:** 19, 20, 117 (bottom); **Virrage Images:** 16 (top); **Vitalii Stock:** 58; **Vladimir Melnikov:** 106; **Vladimir Mulder:** 85 (bottom); **Volodymyr TVERDOKHLIB:** 25 (bottom left); **vvaldmann:** 68; **wavebreakmedia:** 139 (bottom); **Wonchalerm:** 91 (middle); **worradirek:** 49 (top); **WR7:** 90 (bottom); and **Your Hand Please:** 150.

ABOUT ADVENTUREKEEN

We are an independent nature and outdoor activity publisher. Our founding dates back more than 40 years, guided then and now by our love of being in the woods and on the water, by our passion for reading and books, and by the sense of wonder and discovery made possible by spending time recreating outdoors in beautiful places. It is our mission to share that wonder and fun with our readers, especially with those who haven't yet experienced all the physical and mental health benefits that nature and outdoor activity can bring. #bewellbeoutdoors